Operation Highjump

Operation Highjump
The diary of a young sailor
Admiral Byrd's 1946-47 Antarctic Expedition
by Richard J. Miller, S/1AerM

Copyright ©1946-47, ©2011-12

Published and distributed by: Ageless-Sages.com Publishing

PO Box 41
Hinesburg, VT 05461

ISBN 13: 978-0-9815505-2-7
ISBN 10: 0-9815505-2-5
Library of Congress Control Number: 2012933060

Printed in the USA

Newspaper articles reprinted by permission from the Watertown Daily Times

OPERATION HIGHJUMP
Antarctic Expedition, 1946 and 1947

TASK FORCE 68

Table of Contents

Preface

The author of this diary, my father-in-law, is known for his talent in archiving the events of his life and the lives of his loved ones. His bookshelves are filled with photos, newspaper articles and souvenirs from his lifetime of rich experiences. Ric enjoys sharing these events with his family and friends, and a couple years ago, he revealed to me the diary he kept during the Operation Highjump mission to the Antarctic in 1946 and 1947.

After reading a sampling of the diary's entries and looking through its accompanying memorabilia, it occurred to me that our family would be interested in having copies of this journal. Thus began the journey of Ric reading his entries aloud while I typed. We took frequent breaks to look up maps, letters, newspaper articles, etc. After about 2 ½ years, we had the beginnings of the book you now hold in your hands.

Upon researching this mission, I uncovered several theories as to why this mission took place and what was discovered. However, the US Navy reports that Operation Highjump, officially titled The US Navy Antarctic Development Program, 1946-47, had the primary mission of establishing the Antarctic research base Little America IV.

This operation was organized by RADM Richard E. Byrd Jr. USN, (Ret), Officer in Charge, Task Force 68, and led by RADM Richard H. Cruzen, USN, Commanding Officer, Task Force 68, and included 4,700 men, 13 ships, and multiple aircraft.

Ric and I would like to thank his close circle of family and friends who made this publication possible with their insight, expertise, suggestions and support.

I invite you to join the journey and trust you'll enjoy it as much as I have. Ric has captured the essence of this mission-of-a-lifetime through his 19 year-old eyes!

Natalie Tucker Miller

Note: For more information on the mission
visit http://www.ohj.booksforelders.com

Author's Introduction

When in boot camp, sailors take exploratory or comprehensive tests. As a result of the tests, they are assigned someplace within their abilities. There is then an announcement as to where they are going. I went to Lighter-Than-Air school and weather school at Lakehurst NJ.

During the 16-week course, I learned the rudiments of weather. At the end of the course-work a list of possible places where sailors were eligible to go was posted. A sailor would then sign up on the list. When I signed up for my assignment, I thought I ought to do something that I would never get to do again. Thus, I signed up for adventure in the Antarctic with Admiral Byrd.

There are only a certain number of openings, with more people signing up than there are available spots. With only sixteen openings available, the criteria for acceptance included your course-work marks and a very tough physical requirement. The rigors of this assignments included the harsh elements in the Antarctic.

There were other considerations as well. For instance:

- A preference for dark-eyed people to prevent snow blindness.

- A sailor's reaction: We'd never been to sea, we didn't know much, so the mysteries of what we were in for were intriguing. For instance, I didn't know if I was going to be driving dog sleds or what.

From there, I went to Norfolk, Virginia; my first job was to look at the ship in dry dock and be instructed to get a scraper! We had to scrape the bottom of the ship to free it from barnacles and rust, then chip the paint on decks to repaint. We then started out on a two day dry run to see if the ship was in operating condition. This was about six weeks from the time school was out.

Ric "Dick" Miller in Weather School, 1946

In spite of the fact that this is the middle of the 20th century, there was a huge area of the world that was still unknown. If you keep in mind that the area of the US is 3,675,000 sq. miles in area, when you hear that the Antarctic is over 6,000,000 sq. miles, you get a better feel for the size and the challenge that awaited us!

While there had been a number of dog sled explorations to the Antarctic, most of the continent was still unknown and unexplored. The purpose of this expedition was to perform, as complete as possible, aerial mapping of the continent and perhaps just as important, have an opportunity to test both man and equipment under the most adverse possible weather conditions.

With this in mind, and the expertise of Admiral Byrd available as an advisor, the navy put together a more complete group than ever before to explore the continent. With the aid of aerial mapping, we were able to redraw the then present-day maps of the Antarctic. In addition, we discovered many things unknown before, e.g. mountain ranges, inland lakes and so forth. For this purpose the expedition was divided into three parts consisting of the Central, Western and Eastern divisions.

The Central division was to set up camp in the former base called "Little America" which was last used by Admiral Byrd in 1939. From this base, planes were to be sent up to map the area in the vicinity of the South Pole. The Western and Eastern components of the expedition, each having an aircraft tender, an oiler and a destroyer, were to put seaplanes in the water and photograph as much as possible. There was hope that these mappings could be accomplished in a reasonable length of time, but due to very adverse weather conditions, flights could not be sent up as often as desired. Nonetheless, huge amounts of previously unknown territory were mapped.

Considerable information was obtained concerning the use of men and equipment in this adverse climate. It was my great privilege to be part of this important mission.

Richard J. Miller

The USS Pine Island

My ship, the USS Pine Island, was 540' long with a crew of approximately 400.

There was a helicopter deck on the bow. The helicopters were used to observe the ice pack conditions in the area. The stern carried the seaplanes (The USS Pine Island is officially a seaplane tender), which are put in and taken out of the water by crane. There were 3 seaplanes, with 2 operational at all times.

We all slept in compartments 2 and 3 bunks high, with 50 or more men sleeping in the same room. We all had a small locker for our personal items. There was a common shower room, where we took very fast showers. The mess hall had long tables and we ate in shifts, in cafeteria style, to accommodate the whole crew. The food was simple but plentiful. The hangar for the extra seaplane doubled as an activity room. Movies, volley ball, church services and any groups activities took place there.

The book in which the diary entries were discovered.

12 APRIL

102 ND DAY
263 DAYS TO COME
DAY OF WEEK

Today is the Birthday of

April 13   Joyce's Birthday

103 RD DAY
262 DAYS TO COME
DAY OF WEEK

Miss Joyce Carol Whitbeck
17 Fernbank Avenue
Delmar, New York

Today is the Birthday o   April 13   Dad's Birthday

From November 1946 through April 1947, Richard J. Miller went on an adventure that lives only in the imagination of most boys. The following is the transcript of the diary that the 19 year-old sailor kept while serving on the USS Pine Island.

Operation High Jump:

The diary of a young sailor

This book is an unedited transcript of the original diary. We have done our best to preserve the integrity of the author's language, grammar, punctuation and sentiments.

Part One: Stateside

Key: Italicized parenthetical remarks are part of the original script. Non-italicized parenthetical remarks are additions from the author for purposes of clarity.

12 November 1946

Well, leave is over and now the eventful part of my Navy career ought to start shaping up. Bob Dibble, Leo Dephtereos, Bill Austin, Dave Phillips, Ed Gordon, and last but most certainly not least, Milt Pelman made my leaving home almost pleasant. They gave me a royal send off at the station with the singing of Jingle Bells and White Christmas in honor of my future destination, the South Pole. The Navy put me to work immediately loading supplies.

13 November

Our mission (*snow shovels*) can't be very secret because all papers carried an article on it. 13 ships carrying 4000 men to endure harsh weather conditions. We are glad that Admiral Byrd is to be our leader. We move from Portsmouth to NOB (Naval Operations Base) Norfolk and pleaseeee pray that I get off tomorrow to get my seabag before we move.

I lent a fellow my ID and liberty card so he will be caught and I reckon I am going to be in plenty of trouble.

We really worked hard and long. We loaded plenty of supplies down in the lower hatches. It looks like a long voyage.

14 November

Rumor - One of us leaving for a DD and three to the Mt. McKinley, four to the Olympus.

Tried to write letters tonight but gave it up to eat crackers and cheese and to gab with the fellows.

We loaded hundreds of cases of flour, tomatoes, salad oil and shortening on today. We loaded til 5 o'clock and to think that there is supposed to be a shortage of that stuff.

The DD Brownson docked on the next pier with a buddy from Lakehurst.

Spent all AM in NOB looking for seabag. Surprising enough, the seabag is more salty than yours truly because by some mistake it was shipped to a Robert Miller on the USS Wyoming. Ah, well, goodbye to it all.

We loaded a few Christmas trees on board today. It won't be "Christmas in Connecticut" (name of a movie), but it will have a little atmosphere.

15 November

Got special liberty today to go to the Wyoming and get my seabag. As luck would have it, the ship had pulled out. I guess that it's goodbye seabag. I put in a claim but that won't give me the $100 I need to replace my stuff.

Tried to call home at 4 o'clock but no-one answered. I didn't have much to say, anyway.

Took in the movie for the first time in quite a while and we froze sitting on the metal deck. Eddie Cantor was hot.

Cut me paw and got blood on the corpsman's shoe.

Easy day for a change.

16 November

Operation Highjump is real name of expedition.

Had the duty and we had to work after Capt. inspection. I had planned on taking it easy over the wknd. but now that we are still loading supplies, work never stops. Our (*one of them*) helicopter landed on the forward flight deck. I have to stand a 4-8 watch over it tomorrow morning.

I feel a cold coming on but maybe with the help of a blanket of a buddy who is on liberty I'll be able to throw it off.

I went up to the aerological lab for the first time and it looks pretty good. The chief in charge graduated from the advanced class when I came out with class 78. He's a good fellow.

Hand opened up and bled again.

We loaded on Christmas presents for the crew today.

17 November

Day started early, 330, when I went on watch. Boy was it cold standing out there. I went in the plane for a while to keep warm, but it's too risky to stay there. I had my harmonica with me *(I played so bad that it drove me nuts)*. For the books – it's 101 short paces around the flight deck. I didn't get relieved so I missed chow. I really got a cold and I can hardly breathe.

They worked me so much today and inasmuchas I wasn't feeling good, I cussed everyone in the Navy.

I've got a dock watch 4-8 AM on the dock, so I'm going to try to hit the sack early.

We leave for Yorktown tomorrow, so if I get liberty there, I am going to call home and maybe see about sending Bud (Dick's brother) money to go home for Thanksgiving.

18 November

Stood watch in rain from 6-8:20 and didn't get relieved for chow. Didn't bother me because I took it easy the rest of the day. Water was a little rough and me little old stomach jumped a couple of times through my ribs. Watched the helicopter take off a few times and helped with a pibal observation. (A pibal is a small black balloon, about a foot and a half in diameter that you follow in the sky with an instrument called a theodolite. It is used to determine wind velocity and direction.)

For some reason my cold is a might better, but I'll probably lose ground tonight.

We are anchored in some bay near Yorktown where we will proceed tomorrow to load ammo.

Spent most of the PM writing letters because when we leave we'll probably have no mail service and I want to get off as many as possible.

Couldn't buy blankets so I don't know what I'm going to do.

Hope I can get a little liberty in Yorktown to spend me money.

19 November

In spite of all the previous talk on how hard loading ammo is, today was comparatively easy. Except for handling line and taking an end on some 250lb bombs, I rested.

As far as I could see, all that was brought aboard was 100lb, 200lb bombs and some torpedoes.

I found out that there is no liberty here in Yorktown *(actually we are docked at the end of a really long pier and the only house in sight is the Marine Barracks on the hillside)*, but Friday we probably will go back to Portsmouth for a while.

I hope that we get the wknd. off because it would enable me to dash up and see Bud.

Went to the movies. Fred Allen, Jack Benny.

20 November

Today was the last day of handling ammo as far as I was concerned. Since my section had the duty I had to work until 7:30 at night finishing loading torpedo warheads.

With all good intentions of writing letters and doing anything worthwhile, I started back to the compartment. They announced the movie was "Valley of Decision" and soon I found myself sitting through it for the second time *(Greer Garson and Gregory Peck)*.

Today was supposed to be payday but at the last moment they postponed it 'til tomorrow.

<u>21 November</u>

Today they got us up a half hour early to finish with the ammo but I F.O. I worked til 1215 getting all the ship's boats ready for some trial tests today *(Hence I missed payday, but I think there's going to be a stragglers pay in a few minutes)*. We used a Bocush boat to represent a PBM (type of planes carried on the ship) and practiced bringing it in with other boats and taking it up on a crane. It was loads

Loading our PBM's

of fun zipping about the bay in the warm sun and it was associated with the thrill of being raised high in the air by the crane.

Tonight I sure have to write some letters, even if I haven't received any. Someone will have to answer now and then.

22 November

Today was again quite easy. I stood a four hour watch in the morning which got me out of work. At 12 o'clock we brought a PBM on board as practice, and then we put it back in water. We're just making sure that we know how to handle them when the time comes to bring on the three that we are to take on our journey.

(Speaking of the trip, the rumor has it that we'll be back by next summer and that means that I may be able to get leave to go on the canoe trip)

We were supposed to stay on board last night *(sections 2 and 4)* to load gas, but for some reason it was cancelled. I stayed anyway.

23 November

Although we were delayed a few hours from starting liberty because they needed the V (Victor) Division to handle gas, I finally got off ship and made liberty in Norfolk. The late start kept me from going to St. John's (In Annapolis MD) to see Bud. I bunked at the Navy Y and spent most of the first few hours writing letters. I didn't plan on going to Norfolk, so consequently I didn't have anybody to keep me company. *(I went to NOB to check up on my seabag, but the PO was closed. I did go in the ship's service and bought some stuff. A razor, of all things, too.)*

I was tired so I hit the sack early. The dormitory was nice and the sack only cost one half of a rock.

24 November

Got up early enough to attend a breakfast discussion and then they took us to any church we wanted. I went to a little Methodist. Went to an early movie with Bob Hope and got back to the Y in time to feast at a pumpkin pie social.

We sang most of the afternoon and at night there was a dinner discussion. Again, transportation was provided to church. I went to a Presbyterian one that had a fellowship meeting *(with food)* after.

Took in a stay at a USO and then headed back to the Y to pick up my pea coat.

(I called up home Sunday morning and was shocked by the sad news that Grandma Miller had died. I couldn't think of anything appropriate to say).

I got back the PI (Pine Island) about midnight.

25 November

Spent most of the day trying to dodge work, but naturally I got hooked a little.

I got three letters today much to my surprise. Two were from Aud and the other from Mom and Pop. The letter from the folks was very nice, yet terribly sad in that it told of Grandma's death. *(I was the last of our immediate family to talk to her. It was on the last day of my leave and she was feeling bad then. Two days later she died.)*

I pulled a stupid blunder today by sending my undress blue pants to the dry cleaners with a $20 bill in the pocket. Goodbye to that.

Rumor that we're going by way of South America instead of Australia.

26 November

Sent a card to the folks (anniversary).

Got up at 5:30 and we almost literally worked our balls off. We handled 62lb 5 inch shells, 108lb incendiary cases, 110lb 40mm ammunition cases. We (*sections 2 and 4*) worked 'til after 11 o'clock in the evening. It was quite a long day. If my heart doesn't give out, the work won't bother me too much.

Oh yeah, we accomplished a big thing today. I got right up next to the aerological office while we were carrying cases (*That should add the smell of limburger to the reek of sarcasm*).

27 November

We brought on a PBM that is to continue with us on the trip. We expect to take three of them. Today was easy or maybe I was just comparing it to the hard work of yesterday.

I think that I am staying on this ship instead of getting transferred. As far as I know, those leaving are Donald and Ronald Lopp, Lewis Burke and Bill Keyser. They probably go aboard the Mt. Olympus tomorrow or Fri.

My blues came back from the cleaners minus the $20 bill that was in the pocket.

I got to write Phil and Elinor to see if I can help their romance along.

28 November

Thanksgiving. Yup today is Thanksgiving and also my first away from home. It seems strange to eat it in dungarees, but the Navy treated us right for a change and fed us a wonderful meal. Besides two desserts, they also gave everyone a pack of cigarettes.

We worked most of the day putting the wings on the PBM on the overhead of the hangar.

Got off the ship for a minute to go over to see the ice breaker, USS North Wind. It has a bunch of husky dogs on it that we are taking with us. One of them had five little pups.

I've just been informed that I have a 12 to 4 watch in the morning. Yes, we have a lot to be thankful for *(it could be 8 hours)*.

All other sections, besides 4, had liberty from Wed. night to Fri. morning.

29 November

In a way, today was almost ideal. I not only got a pair of purloined dungarees, but I got my whole seabag. I heard that the Wyoming was in port so I carried some junk off the ship and dashed over to it. Sure enough, the postmaster had it right there and soon I was carrying it off the ship.

I didn't work much all day because there wasn't much doing. We did take on two more PBMs and a Soc *(small sea plane)* which kind of leaves our aft flight deck crowded. The wings hung over the side.

Went up to the air station at Norfolk *(with D.C. Lopp)* in order to see some of the boys that graduated with us in class 78. They were on liberty so we took in a movie.

30 November

They double crossed me again and made me stay late again on the weekend. We had to help the duty section fasten down the planes and as a result I couldn't get to Annapolis to see Bud.

Bought a camera at the S.S. (ship's store) and later after trying a bunch of stores found out I couldn't get film.

Got a bunk at the Y and after the usual bumming around I played handball and saw the "Outlaw."

1 December

Went to a Lutheran church in the morning after "breakfast club". Called the folks for the last time and even talked to Dave Harris (a good friend of Bud's).

I saw "The Road to Utopia" which I had missed when it played at Lakehurst.

As usual I filled myself with cake and cookies at the Y luncheon *(I'd like to say the Y has done a great deal for the boys during and after the war)*.

Had a supper discussion and then went to First Presbyterian church young folks meeting. Oddly enough they offered a prayer for the boys going to the Antarctic. More cake and stuff followed by yummmmmmmmmmm.

2 December

Pulled in at two o'clock am from the weekend which was my last liberty in the states.

At 1 o'clock pm, with more than the usual number of photographers and with a few friends and relatives of the boys on the dock, we pulled out. The ocean has been quite rough so my stomach has been doing more loops than a circus performer.

At 5 o'clock I went on my 1st aerology watch and it wasn't too bad. We only had to take a few hourly observations and then we knocked off at midnight.

All of the photographers tried to get us to wave and smile as they took our pictures when we were pulling away from the dock. I'm afraid we weren't too good subjects because all they got was a few half hearted waves and not many more movie smiles.

3 December

If I had written the next two pages on time all that I would have been able to put down would be OOOOOOOOOOOOOOOOO. I was quite sick and that is no joke. I really fed the fish.

We've been traveling down the 75th meridian almost due south. The latitude changes about every 5 hours. The average speed has been a little better than 15 knots. 5-12pm watch.

4 December

The part about being sick goes for today, too. No breakfast, no dinner, had supper, then lost supper ☺. After the last mishap I felt quite a bit better so 2 /class AerM (aerographer's mate) Powers, and myself left Simpson at the lab and went to see "Meet Me in St. Louis" again.

Our speed picked up to 17.5 knots because we want to get to Panama early to fix one of the plane motors that broke when the plane broke loose in the storm yesterday.

Chief Bailey *(who was in the advanced class at Lakehurst when we were there)* let us knock off at 1100. Good to get the sleep.

5 December

The ship has started having whites (a morning announcement indicates which uniform is to be worn that day) for the uniform of the day *(already I've lent two pairs of pant to those who were lacking)*.

Saw some porpoises and flying fish jumping in the water off the port beam. That's a good sign that we are in southern waters. We saw land on both sides which means we are passing through some of the Caribbean *(West Indies)* straits *(later I found out that is was between Espanol and Cuba)*.

We're doing 18 knots, worked 8-5:30.

Took a pibal and helped with a Radiosonde (measurements). Everything was screwed up, but it will straighten out.

6 December

Nothing special happened today. I worked from 8 until 12 at night. It acted as a kind of sample of the hours we will have when we get busy on taking weather observations for official records.

7 December

Today has been different for a change. We saw land all morning and at 1200 we started through the canal (Panama). It's after 6 now, and we still aren't through. In general the scenery is quite beautiful. A good share of the time we have thick jungle on both sides and every now and then we come to small settlements *(mostly for canal workers)* the canal consists of three sets of locks. The first, raising you into a nice freshwater lake, which to me was similar to some of those I saw on my canoe trips. I thought we would have mail call today but I guess not. Saw lots of palms of all kinds and tropical birds. Every now and then gun emplacements can be seen, which gives the impression of wartime security.

Took off two PBMs today with the usual amount of confusion. We just left the canal. Balboa and Panama City are to our left.

8 December

Last night we got our first liberty in Panama. We visited the city of Panama and it really showed evidence of having been a Navy liberty town. There are dozens of taxi drivers etc. who propositioned us at every turn. The liberty was only for 3 hours but I wasn't too sorry to go back.

Today I spent most of the day holding a fire hose while we took on 100 octane gas. I got a little sun burned because the thermometer hit 92 degrees. We fooled around the office til 10:30, and secured. It was the first time I hit the sack before 12 in quite a while.

The North Wind tied up on the other side of the pier and I saw Burke and Keyser but I couldn't get their attention. *(I found out that the submarine, The Sennet, is going too).*

9 December

Worked to 12am trying to get helium bottles out of the hold (below decks) but we weren't very successful without the automatic hoist.

Pipenbrink, Burke and I went on liberty in the afternoon and enjoyed swimming at the Balboa Clubhouse. I was impressed by the way young kids of about 6 years of age could swim and dive. They made me look foolish. We met Simpson and all went off taking pictures and seeing the sights. After eating and trying out my Spanish on the Panamanian waitress, we headed again for Panama City.

Miller, Simpson, Burke

We visited a lot of souvenir shops and about all I saw that I wanted was an alligator handbag that mom might like. It only cost $25.00 and they could probably be talked down to $20.00. I might get one on the way back.

We met Keyser and all went to the Missouri Burlesque til time to get back.

<u>10 December</u>

Was up to the office at 6 as usual. Either Pipenbrink or I gave the altimeter setting wrong to the PBM pilot and when he landed his altimeter said 200 feet above the sea *(he was mad and I'll sure be careful if it was me)*.

They tried bringing the PBM back on board today *(they took them off so they wouldn't hit going through the canal)*. They screwed it up as usual. Something was always wrong. If it wasn't the motors of the boats *(that bring the plane close the ship)* breaking down, or the power of the ship shutting off, it was the crane breaking down.

For a change I don't work at night and now maybe I can get some of my own work done. I've got letters to write, clothes by the bushel and stenciling to do.

My aerological office and group. Standing: Pipenbrink, LeGrande, Ens. Huscke   Sitting: Miller, Chief Bailey

11 December

Yesterday we crossed the equator and I'm sure I'll remember it for quite a while. Ceremonies started at 1630 and lasted all night. Some of the things we had to do were really funny. I had to get up in front of the gang while another fellow danced. They had us on our hands and knees yelling "Allah to the Shellbacks!", "Goodie! Tomorrow I'll be a Shellback", "I'm a slimy polliwog,

The boys who did the initiating at the equator

honorable Shellback sir!" For the least little thing they would belt us, and even for nothing at all. I literally got a bitty bang out of it when they ran us through the gauntlet.

12 December

Woke up again in the aerology shack a little stiff after sleeping on the deck. The word came over the loud speaker, that due to the damage caused by the fire, continuation of the ceremonies was impossible *(because they needed men)* and that we were all Shellbacks.

I had a little run in with Razavich because I guess I stuck my nose in his work *(he's AERM 1ˢᵗ class)*.

We broke 3 Radiosonde balloons trying to get them off in the heavy wind.

I got the package from home with a lot of clothes in it that won't do me much good.

We have a chance to send Christmas Telegrams home. I may.

13 December

Today was quite long for me. I carried 100lb sacks of flour and potatoes all day long. I think I strained my right shoulder a little. At 430 I went on aerology watch which lasted until twelve.

Again today we saw schools of flying fish that were stirred up by the splash of our bow cutting the water.

I sent the telegram. The best in Season's Greetings from the equator. By the time they get it, I won't be any place near there, but it was a thought.

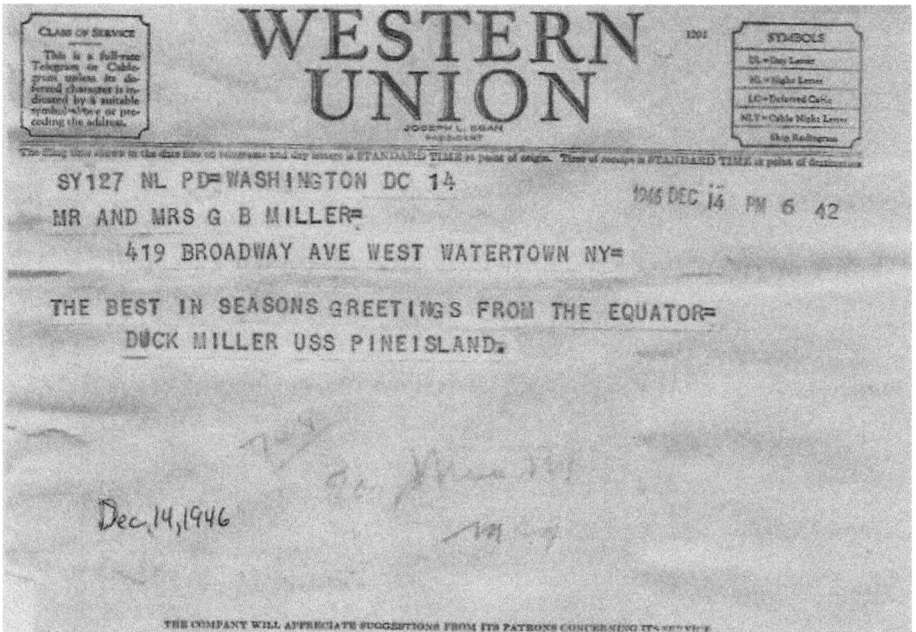

14 December

The plan for the day was Captain's inspection of dungarees and then holiday routine. Per usual it didn't apply to little Richard. After working a couple of hours at the office this morning I went on the flour line again. I carried 20 bags of flour (*one ton*) through a few compartments, ten bags of coffee *(500 lbs)* etc.. In the afternoon while most of the fellows were in their sacks, I carried 29 bags *(a ton and a half)*.

Remember how I used to make paste with flour and water? That's how I felt when I sweated today. By the end of the day I was getting a little pale *(like a snowman)*.

No watch tonight so I'll wash clothes and go to the movies. Second time since we left the states.

15 December

Today I wasn't mad at anything or anybody. I actually had the day off perhaps my last 'til after we start back. I went to church and there were quite a number there compared to when we were in port. They even had a small hand organ.

Simpson and I spent part of the afternoon taking pictures and the rest laying *(or is it lying)* in the sun. The sun wasn't too hot but it was comfortable basking there on deck.

I've been reading a book all evening and it's been a grand feeling having nothing on my mind.

Right now everyone is around shooting the breeze before taps.

16 December

The watch all day and then 'til 12 at night came my way again. I didn't mind it too much because I wrote a couple of letters and took in the movie. If I'm not being too dramatic, I'd say that the letters were my last connection with the outside world *(anything that isn't associated with Pine Island)* because the mail service closed at 6:00 this morning.

There are rumors that we may drop a party on an island to establish a radio and weather station if it is true I'll ask for it. The temperature didn't go above 70 and I figured that we were supposed to be at the warmest latitude in the world at this time of year.

Finished the book "Gorilla" and I'm now on "God's Little Acre" *(not literally)*.

17 December

I knocked off work at 1600 today. Did I say work? Well, I spent most of the day finishing "God's Little Acre." I fell asleep reading because I didn't have much sleep last night. I must be out of training because in civilian life I went for weeks with less than 5 hours sleep a night. Besides that, I went to school, worked, ran track, played in the handball tournament and besides that I found time to work on the Minstrel show-my social life-and homework.

We refueled on the move today and it's quite a trick to keep the ships side by side and have the oil line come over without getting in some kind of trouble. I was mad because I didn't take any pictures of it.

18 December

Today some of the boys started getting their fall weather gear. There sure is a mess of it. They issue sweaters just like the ones the folks sent from home. I'm kinda worried they might think it's theirs and not let me keep it.

Saw Jack Oakey in "On Stage, Everybody." It's old and stunk.

All I did today was take a couple of pibal observations. I'm not so hot at it because I could never pick up the balloon in my theodolite and had to have help on it. It's tougher than on land because the roll of the ship makes the balloon bounce out of sight.

As you can see by the lack of news, it was just a day of relaxation for me.

19 December

We again went through the traditional Navy game of "Which Size Do You Want" and then you gaze upon a monstrosity pair of pants that only a giant could use. What I'm referring to is the issuance of foul weather gear. I admit the Navy provided pretty well this trip. I'd like to keep some of the stuff they gave me. Here's the list: One pair rain pants, one pair foul weather pants, one rain jacket, one foul weather jacket, three large pairs of wool socks, four pairs of gloves, one pair of arctic shoes, one pair of arctic overshoes, one hat, two sets of long underwear, one pair of wind goggles, one pair of sun glasses, one seabag, one heavy wool sweater.

Some guys got even more because they'll stand watches on deck. They got heavy, fur lined parkas that were keen.

Had the watch til 12 at night.

20 December

Friday is the day that everything is supposed to sparkle in this man's Navy (the day they shine the brass). Yup, every ship, land station and dog house has field day. We spent most of the am scrubbing down the office and pibal shack.

In the afternoon we took a pibal sounding. I surprised myself by picking it up but I lost it after the 5th minute. We got the 6th reading from Pipenbrink (Pi).

One of the strikers (someone who has not been to weather school but is learning on the job) in the office *(McCay)* is going up for his rate soon.

Simpson is finally going to get off mess cooking and is going back to work in the office. We need him because there is going to be a good deal of work from now on.

We are nowhere near land and we have birds following us *(albatross)*.

21 December

At the movies last night they showed pictures of the Antarctic. It included photos of thousands of penguins on land that we are supposed to go near.

After 11 o'clock today we had holiday routine. I hit the sack at 1230 and just got up in time for chow. Also saw "The Tiger Woman." For a change, the movies were really packed and I had to sit in the second balcony. I say second balcony but it really is a catwalk that runs along the bulkhead of the hangar.

We had a surprise inspection and I got balled out for wearing work shoes *(slightly unpolished)* with undress blues.

It got cold enough to wear my foul weather jacket this evening.

22 December

Yes, today we started our full weather observations. My section of Chief Bailey, LeGrande, Pipenbrink and myself went on at 0800 and got off at 1930. Ordinarily we should get off at 2000 but the next watch relieved us in time to go to the movies *(had to sit on the deck because they wouldn't let us on to the catwalk)*.

All of the lookouts are peering carefully into the distance. The Captain has promised a fruitcake to the first man who spots an iceberg. Even the officers on the bridge have their old binoculars pointed towards the horizon.

The Ensign in our office claimed he spotted spouting whales.

23 December

8 to 8 as usual. We got a little surprise today by being presented with the news that we would be able to mail letters 'til 0700 tomorrow. I resolved to write a goodly number of letters before the deadline. When I got off work, what did I do? Write letters? Nope. I went to the movies *(such willpower)* to see my boy Roy Rogers *(of all things)*. Result: Just one letter.

We were all supposed to have our mugs snapped with foul weather gear on but we were just too busy to go down.

No ice sighted as. Maybe because the water temperature is 42°.

Part Two: "Iceberg off Starboard Bow"

24 December

The Chaplain passed out Christmas presents to everyone.

Today brought a few changes in the usual run of things. The ship took a sharp list to the right when the loud speaker boomed "Iceberg off starboard bow." It wasn't too big but as the day progressed and the ceiling lifted more and more, larger ones were sighted.

We refueled the Brownson, and we saw Caldwell. As I talked to him, rather yelled across to the ship, our first snow fall came. Lightly first and then rather heavy.

Thanks to the Chaplain we had a Christmas Eve celebration. We sang Christmas songs. The Pine Island Penguins tooted out with a few pretty good numbers. Our South Pole Santa *(dressed in foul weather clothes)* kept us in stitches and bid Merry Christmas to all and to all good night.

25 December

Yup, Christmas Day found yours truly working my usual shift from 8 to 8. I couldn't make church services because of the watch but most of the ship was on holiday routine.

I did make it down for the Christmas dinner like the one we had on Thanksgiving, it was really scrumptious. Trays were literally heaped so much that you actually couldn't even see the tray. There was almost two layers on every tray. I ate so much that I could barely move. I'll save the menu so I'll be able to remember all we had.

We've been at a standstill for almost 12 hours. There is ice on three sides of us and the only way out is the way we came in.

All of the plane crews are going to put in 12 hours flying tomorrow while they fly 1500 miles each to look over the lay of the ice.

26 December

Ice was really thick about the ship today. It was small pack ice with only about 18 inches deep. Amid the ice, though, was a huge iceberg whose size one cannot picture unless he has been close to one. We practiced with our five inch gun by firing a few rounds at it. Two thirds of them hit.

All of the day's flights that were scheduled were cancelled due to the aerological officer's weather forecast. One plane was put over the sides but it was injured in the fuel operation. They had me running up to the Captain every 10 minutes with the wind speed and direction.

Today we broke 3 pibal and 2 Radiosonde balloons. We are going to run out of helium I can see that.

Hit the usual trail to the movies.

27 December

The Commodore was really anxious to get a flight off today. I guess he wanted to fly over to the Brownson for some reason. Flying was virtually impossible though, because we had a ceiling of only 500 feet and poor visibility. To top it all, heavy fog rolled in making the ceiling 0 and 1/32 of a mile visibility.

During the day the Commodore and few other big brass came in the office while I was the only one there. I was working on a Radiosonde chart and didn't know they were there until someone yelled "Attention!" He talked to me natural like and asked me what kind of weather we were going to have. I told him all I could which wasn't much and no doubt he went away dissatisfied.

28 December

The Commodore seems to be getting a little impatient about getting some flights off. I guess that is one of the main reasons we headed north. He thinks that there are too many hunks of ice combined with fog down here. The ceiling was 0 and the visibility 1/32 of a mile for a while again.

George Razavich AERM 1/C (1st class), who works in our office got a little publicity from Ernie Pyle. Ernie had a paragraph about Raz in his book "Brave Men." It gave a good description of Raz and his betting tendencies. The first part of the book was written on Raz's ship during the invasion of Sicily.

29 December

Went through the line for pancakes twice this AM. It was rather a big day for the flyboys. The aerological forecast that our fog would lift and flight conditions would be possible. They sweated the forecast out and sure enough the ceiling and visibility went up to 1400 and 12 miles respectively. They had me sending up ceiling balloons all day and at 1700 we were able to take our first pibal in days. We got the first plane off in the morning and as we were working on the second, word came over the loud speaker that George I was over the continent *(the first plane of this task force)*. Our Commodore was anxious to beat the Currituck's planes.

They rolled the boys out for flight quarters at 2330. I stayed in my rack, legally for a change.

30 December

Again at 0400 they broke up the boys sleep with flight quarters as George II returned to the ship. Most of the fellows only had about 3 hours sleep all night.

If a stranger came aboard this ship he couldn't help but notice the tension that prevails at the thought of possible disaster. (Sea planes were called George I, II and III. George I has disappeared and they're not sure where it is, they figure it has crashed on the continent). We lost radio connection with the plane at 5 this morning and nothing else has been heard from them since. Now *(9:30pm)* they are 8½ hours overdue. We've been hoping against hope that the plane was forced to land on water *(for at the time they last reported, they were over a bay near the continent)* to wait out the weather. They only had gas 'til 900 tonight, so they can't be cruising around in the air.

31 December

18 hours the plane is overdue and still the weather hasn't cleared up so we can send out a search plane. The missing plane is doubly important because, you see, it has the Captain of our ship aboard. He was going along to observe the ice conditions. You can see why everyone is a little glum. One of the crew members slept underneath me and the other, beside me. Tisn't pleasant to think of what may have happened.

(24 hours later and still no word).

My department head, LT Oller, is making it a little hard for us because he has a lot of worries. Everyone seems jumpy.

They planned a good New Year's celebration, but for obvious reasons, it has been postponed. As usual, I took in a movie.

1 January 1947

In place of all (New Year's) celebration we had a prayer service for the crew and the captain in the missing plane. For a while the weather cleared up and we almost got a search plane off but the fog socked in again and we brought it back on board. (PBM's were put in the water by crane). It was holiday routine today so most of the ship stayed in their racks. We had another big meal in the same style as the Thanksgiving Day and Xmas meals. I did justice to it and again feel uncomfortably full.

I hope someone tells me when Lent starts so I can give up something. I haven't got the will power to deny it to me for a whole year, like in a New Year's resolution so I just do without if for six weeks.

2 January

They rolled us out at 0200AM and had us up all night. The PBM that we had secured to the fantail ran afoul of the port boom and ripped its port wing. Ironically enough as soon as both of our remaining planes were indisposed, so to speak, the fog lifted. We had over 12 hours of good flying weather. God help the missing crew if they needed help from us.

Today and yesterday found the temperature to be over 40 degrees. If this is even a little example of the Antarctic I certainly think it was overestimated. I know that it is a lot colder at home. To help the day along with a little interest I perceived with my own eye, one of the little things that the Antarctic is famous for. That's right, a penguin. They're just little fellows, and the one I saw was swimming beside the ship. We are 300 miles from land so I wonder where his relatives are. I guess that he came out on some ice flow.

3 January

Situation all remains the same but as you can see the days are flying along. Saw my first seal today on a small ice berg that floated by. Later in the trip if it can possibly be arranged I hear a seal hunting party is going to be organized. Purely scientific of course.

Admiral Byrd is probably now on his way down here. The Philippine Sea *(carrier)* is bringing a few land planes *(DC 30's I guess)* to be used on the airstrip that is to be built at Little America (the base on the continent). They will take off the carrier with aid of Jado *(jet)* and will remain here until they are discarded.

<u>4 January</u>

If I came from Texas or Oklahoma I'd say "I been a-readin things today." I finished Drag Harlan, Freedom Road, and Lassie Come Home. Picked up a broadcast from the Mt. Olympus that was going back to the states. We have a radio in the office on which we can get broadcasts from the states now and then. They said that the Mt. Olympus had been ice bound for 5 days and they were being amused by the seals and the penguins on the ice flow near-by. Speaking of seals, I saw my second one today.

No word from the missing plane. We have George III making a practice hop after being laid up since we got here. We got our highest Raysonde sounding so far today. It was 76 contacts 84 mil 66,000 ft. the balloon broke at that height (Raysonde is an electronic box which measures temperature, pressure and humidity. It's a radio that sends the information back in a code that has to be interpreted).

<u>5 January</u>

Well, my Navy career is 10/24ths done. Yes, last night completed my 10th month and I almost think it has seemed that long.

They called flight quarters at 10am this morning. George III made two short practice hops and fixed the little items

39

that needed correction. At 1930 tonight the commodore and the doc boarded the plane and we thought that they finally were on their way to search for the missing flyers and the captain. They got 40 miles and turned back because of SW (storm and weather). We hope to try again tomorrow.

I tried my hand at ping-pong tonight but was beaten 21-12 third time I've been beaten in the Navy. Gee gosh, I tell you I was out of practice etc.

6 January

Today I'm happy to say marked the first time that we have gotten away a plane to carry on an intensive search for the missing plane. I'd like to add that it's about time. If I ever get forced down in a plane and have to depend on the PI (Pine Island is the name of the ship we were on) for a rescue, I think that I will grab a 45 and shoot myself so as not to prolong the agony.

They have kept us hopping sending messages every ½ hour and doing all the little things that go to make up a striker's toil (*such as cleaning gear*).

I think that I can die happy now, I've seen about all that (there is to) the Antarctic. I saw my first whale today although it was from a distance.

<u>7 January</u>

For a while today we had two planes in the air but they both came back with some kind of trouble.

The Brownson (destroyer) and the Canisteo (oiler) both came alongside today to transfer supplies. We got 26 more helium bottles to add to our fast diminishing supply. Guess who handled them. The Brownson wasn't quite close enough to see Caldwell (a friend from Lakehurst), though.

The fellows are going to take their Aerm 3/c (third class petty officer) test tomorrow and I guess two of them will be rated. I am going to take it with them, just to see how I can do. I won't even have my time in for over 4 months so I'm not worried about the test because my mark won't count. It's going to be a long time before I get a rate even though I know this stuff.

<u>8 January</u>

We took the test this evening and it was a toughie. There were some questions I looked at with a blank stare such as define histerisis and paradoxas (*I shot some bull but found out later that neither of them were right*)

This is probably the last time I'll be on a ship where there is an opening for Aerographers 3rd.

Mr. Oller (a LT. senior grade who was our weather officer aboard the ship) got on my fanny for eating too much and too often during working hours. If I could get off watch to go to church maybe I would find out when Lent started so I could give up such stuff.

I'm getting real used to this life and it doesn't bother me now.

9 January

Today Mr. Oller said that he would hardly feel justified if he rated any of the fellows because the test marks were so low. Personally, I think we're all qualified. Today was quite slow and for quite a while I amused myself by working out algebra problems from an old book I found in the office. I was stumped by the reduction of square root in factoring. It's something we never covered in school.

We tried to get a plane off again but it started gathering ice at 400 ft, which is very rare, so it turned back.

These PBM's sure aren't the type of work planes for rugged duty like this. We're having a heavy snowstorm now.

10 January

Today we got the test results; my luck was a little better than usual due to my pre-test brush up and therefore I managed to come out on the top by a slight margin.

Mr. Oller said that he would try to get Mac (*another striker*) rated this quarter for certain reasons and the other fellows the next quarter. I still won't have my time in.

Today was nice and quiet and I almost enjoyed it. We didn't have much to do but it's getting to be a standing joke that we never remember to time check the instruments.

The sea got choppy but there was no swell to make the ship roll. I never felt much better. In spite of the fact that we had to work faster than the devil today because we had two search planes in the air.

Part Three: Good News, Bad News

<u>11 January</u>

The news today was both good and bad. The ship practically went wild with the receipt of the message form one of the planes. It read "Mariner George I sighted. Live men near-by." It was follow by "Six men alive by our count. Three men, Henderson, RM 1/c, Lopez, ENS, and now Williams, mechanic 1/c, killed in crash. All others including the skipper of the ship are well enough to walk. (This information written on wing of crashed plane) They had no radio communication between the planes, nor could the sea plane land to get verbal information from the crew).

The guy who bunked near me was killed (*Williams*).

We (G-3) dropped them all kinds of supplies including whiskey.

SOUTH POLE EXPEDITION 1946-47

One of the sad parts of the rescue

12 January

The survivors were brought aboard later this AM. There were 6 altogether and some of them really looked beat. One fellow was taken out of the plane on a stretcher and they took him by where I was standing trying to get some pictures. It was the pilot and his face was a horrible mass of burns. It was much worse than it would have been under ordinary conditions because of inattention. The skipper has a broken nose and another had a broken arm. The others were just cut up a bit.

The plane was flying beneath the clouds and the pilot was blinded by snow causing the plane to nick the top of a hill. The plane was still under control when it exploded 20 ft above the ground. It broke in three places and somehow the prop ripped apart the middle sector tearing apart two men. A third had the back of his head cut off (the *one who slept near me*). He was beyond help and died in the snow two hours later. The survivors were blown clear of the plane and landed in the soft snow. They lived in the tail section of the plane with the supplies they were able to save. They buried the pieces of the bodies nearby in the snow and spent 13 days in the wreckage. G-3 landed in the water 8 miles away and the men walked to the shore almost getting lost due to blinding storm. Sled tracks of the rescue party guided them back. They were paddled to the waiting plane in a rubber raft. The survivors never gave up hope or they probably would have died.

13 January

The rest of the ship had their holiday routine as per usual the Aerographers sat in their office. The holiday was a delayed New Year's celebration that was held in the place of the one that wasn't held (*get that double talk, will ya?*) because the flyers were missing. I did get off to go to church for the first time since we left the states.

They had the usual holiday meal, although it wasn't quite up to snuff it satisfied my meager desires.

I found an old "*Owl*" (A high school magazine) *in* my locker that I must have stowed away in Norfolk. I enjoyed reading it again.

I was all set for a nice evening rest and had two blankets pulled over me in order to get rid of my cold when over the loud speaker came "Fire fire fire in the magazine." Well, with tons of ammunition aboard and thousands of gallons of 100 octane gas we ran, and I wasn't but ½ dressed when I got to my post. Later it turned out that someone just shot of a firecracker in the magazine.

14 January

Today some fool poured gas in the scupper. The guys don't seem to use their heads *(the scupper is the drain on the weather deck and guys sometimes toss cigarettes there)*. This ship is the most dangerous one in the fleet and if anyone should touch off any of the hot stuff we wouldn't be able to survive in these icy waters even if we did get clear. Everyone is kind of jittery on that account and we sleep with our foul weather clothes by our bed so we can get off quickly. I was assigned to life raft 11 with 16 others today. I went down to see it and all there was there was a life preserver.

Piepenbrink (Pi), the other fella on watch with me, has just been assigned to department cleaner *(I was lucky not to get it, but I may in a month or so)*. And our chief is sick. That leaves just the 2nd class and myself to handle the day watch. We're going to be quite busy I guess.

15 January

Aujourd'hui il fait tres quiet. I held down the office in the afternoon. (*The chief was there but he was either sleeping or working on his hobby so he wasn't much help*). Le Grande took a well deserved afternoon off. I was relieved at 6:30 pm.

The sea has been quite rough due to 25 knot wind so I'm beginning to feel that feeling again. I played a little ping pong tonight and found that I still retained a little of the ability after all.

I finished "You Don't Live Forever" and John Steinbeck's "Pastures of Heaven."

16 January

One year ago today, Bob and I went down to take an Army physical. They said I had a slight murmur.

For a change, this part of the aerology department had a real easy day. The Raysonde receiver was out of commission so there was very little to do at the office. In as much as Le Grande had yesterday afternoon off, the chief and I flipped a coin to see who would have this PM off. I don't think the chief was happy with the result.

I finally got around to washing one of the two sets of whites that I got dirty in Panama. Luckily I got out of a bag inspection today because I was on watch so I want to be prepared if I get hooked again.

The latest rumor is that we are going to have to stay here an extra month because we are behind schedule and only have two planes.

17 January

The Brownson is due to take our mail off tomorrow and since we don't get such an opportunity very often, I spent a good share of the day writing. I wrote at least 17 letters. I wrote them all on watch so as anyone could assume I wasn't too busy.

Miller on watch

I got a hold of complete list of the ship's compliment from Mr. Huscke. I almost fainted when I found out there is another fellow from H2O town (Watertown, NY, where Dick is from) on board. His handle is Bob Benjamin of the Second Division. I'll look him up tomorrow. It's funny that I could go this long before I found out such a thing.

<u>18 January</u>

Mail went off at 630 this morning to the Brownson. Along with the mail we transferred 5 of our now famous survivors. (*The only one who didn't go was the skipper*) And their destination will be the US. One of the boys, Lt. LeBlanc, is in a bad way. He doesn't know it now but he will lose an arm, both feet and one eye. Besides that, he'll have to undergo months of surgery to restore his face. It's been snowing continuously all day and with the help of fog the visibility has been 1/16th of a mile. We passed by several large ice bergs today. They are a beautiful blue white that would make good color shots if we ever had a little sun.

<u>19 January</u>

With some little incidents such as happened today, I don't find it hard to write a little account of the day's events. The helicopter took off this AM with the commodore on board and as it was coming for a good landing there was a slight explosion that sent the rotors in all directions. (*I have a small piece but I'll probably lose interest and throw it away*). The copter just dropped easily into the slightly chilly water to give the pilot and the commodore their Sunday morning bath. Neither were hurt. I rushed out to watch the plane sink when Mr. Oller came in and yelled "Take a special" (go cover for somebody) , so I didn't see everything. A few minutes late I went out to take some pictures. They had the plane ½ out of the water on a crane and as I waited for the rest to be lifted out then it dropped and went to the deep 6. Sniff, no pictures.

20 January

From now on most of my writing will be concerned with what has happened from 7pm to 7am. Yup we switched watches after 4 weeks of operation and I now work the graveyard shift. I like the watch better in some ways but it does have its disadvantages. We can't hit the rack (go to bed) til 8:15 because we have to go to quarters and from then on its quite hard to get my sleep because of all the racket in the sleeping compartment. Besides if we want to get enough sleep we have to sleep through the noon meal which is the best of the day.

The watch is quieter without the officers running in and out so that leads to more freedom. I notice for the first time that we have a short period where there isn't much sunlight.

21 January

For the second day in a row that clang clang clang of the general alarm has dragged me out of the sack and sent me to my battle station. Of course they are only drills but it sure does cut into my sleep. On watch for a change I was really kept hopping. Alright so I did put down the book I was reading to answer the buzzer. Le Grande is studying for his first class exam and shouldn't be disturbed too much. The wind went up to 29 knots and the sea and swell got quite bad. It didn't bother my landlubber stomach a bit even if we did have greasy pork chop sandwiches for night rations.

22 January

Pulled out of the rack again at 1430. This time it was for abandoned ship drill. Believe me I think I'll choose to go down comfortably with the ship instead of hanging on to a life raft with 16 others. You're going to die either way, so maybe I can get into the galley and eat myself to death.

Speaking of food, for night rations we had steak sandwiches and a huge can of fruit salad for three of us. Ate so much I'm lucky if I don't die with fruit baskets hanging from my ears.

I was reading in the daily press where our CV, the Philippine Sea, also lost a helicopter. We're still ahead with one of them and a plane.

23 January

They say that the aerologists FO'd this time. We got two flights out over the continent and we've had to really be on our toes sending and receiving messages concerning them. *(After the rush was over I counted 40 some messages that the three of us had sent out.)* It, in addition to our regular work, made time fly almost as fast as my hair is falling out. Saw on a message that came in that the MT Olympus has made a landing in the vicinity of Little America. I don't know whether I'm glad not to be with them or not. The chances were 1 in 4 I would be but I lost out. It's going to be tough going home and saying after being this close that I was never on the continent.

24 January

Yippee! I'm a rootin' tootin' two gun man who yearns for the west. I just finished Zane Grey's thrilling westerner "Dessert Gold."

In the Pine Knot (our newspaper), the news is that due to a certain ice pack, Admiral Cruzen thinks that some of the metal hulled ships may have to return to the U.S. sooner than expected. If anyone stays, it will probably be us and the Currituck because we can lay off the ice packs and still operate with our planes. Besides, I like it here and I don't want to leave. (*Yegads and they drag him off in a straight jacket*).

The skipper came into the office and congratulated us on the good work we did during yesterday's flight operations.

25 January

A long but easy night again found me ready for the rack. Today we had a beautiful sunset where a solid red sky (*well ½ of it*) colored a layer of strato-cumulus in a sight to behold. That died out in a very few minutes; the picture was the same only this time it was caused by the sunrise. We are now having a few minutes of twilight which will gradually increase in length til the well known Antarctic winter sets in.

We just got a bit of bad news from the MT Olympus that told us a couple more men were killed during their landing operations. I guess there'll be more sad people in the States.

26 January

Every night just before taps the chaplain offers a little prayer over the loud speakers. It's usually pretty good and no matter what his religion everyone stops what he is doing and bows his head. (*We all get a big kick out of it when the Bosun (boatswain) follows him a minute later.*) His raspy voice replaces the chaplain's mellow voice with "Taps Taps." It kind of gets you back in that navy mood.

We drew cards to see who would secure early last night because there wasn't much doing. It ended up that I was in my rack by 4am. I should be getting thinner because I've missed 4 meals in a row and I intend to sleep through the next.

27 January

Being on the night watch we could laugh at the day watch as they struggled with helium bottles (*they got 20 of them from the Canisteo which refueled us yesterday*). We are now proceeding in company with the Canisteo to Peter the First Island. (*YeGads! You mean to tell me we might even see a piece of land before this cruise is done?*) I don't know why we are going there, but I guess the officers will end up by going seal hunting. As an excuse for this sport they'll probably say the ship needs fresh meat.

We picked up an armed services broadcast from the States and it came in pretty good. It lasted for hours although I only tuned in a little while because I was busy but Red Skelton brought back memories.

<u>28 January</u>

We didn't make Peter the 1st because we ran into high winds (*guess who first noticed them?*) and had to change course to reduce the strain on the aircraft.

Today they broke us out of the rack by yelling "Collision!" over the loud speakers. I do wish they'd yell "Drill!" first. Le Grande and I exchanged duties at the office. He took the observations and did the dirty work while I worked up the Raysonde charts, Prudo charts and handled the logs. I had it easy, only he secured early (*like I usually do*) and left me to hold down the office until the day watch relieved us.

We got shitty sandwiches for night rations so I'm starving, almost literally (*since I haven't eaten for almost a day*).

<u>29 January</u>

The rumor has it that we can't get to Peter the 1st Island because it's frozen in. I doubt it. They had us dragged out of our sacks for a General Quarters drill aujourd'hui. We are always getting our sleep disturbed.

I just got thinking we could get a good basketball team out of the enlisted personnel in aerology. Here is the reason.

Pipenbrink,	6'2"
Simpson	6'1"
Razevich	6'1"
LeGrande	6'0"
Miller	5'10" (*shorty ain't I?*)

It's a pretty good average for 8 guys. This writer (*Jack Case in person*) thinks. (Jack Case was the sports editor for the Watertown Daily Times. He had his name on every sports page during the war.)

30 January

Up as usual during my sleeping hours. This time it was a fire drill. Finished Zane Grey's Shadow of the Tail and have started Prairie Guns. It's my education (*alright so it's relaxing*). But I'm afraid mon frère wouldn't appreciate it.

I played the chief a couple of games of chess. He did me dirt in the first one. But I managed to force him to a stale mate in the second. I reckon that I just ain't no good.

I saw some pictures of the new mountain range when I was at my fire watch. They looked like some drifts that the wind blows up back home. (The planes mapping the continent photographed a new mountain range.)

31 January

We broke three Raysonde balloons trying to get it off in high winds, but tonight we had no mishap. We always seem to find some night wanderer who is fascinated by the huge balloon and who goes out his way for the chance to assist us. (Raysonde balloons are about six feet in diameter and carry the instruments aloft until the balloon bursts.)

This ends the first full month down here and now that I look back it wasn't too bad (*It only had a little excitement to keep the ships young blood churning*).

I got a big kick out of the fact that in North America the temperature got to 78.8 degrees below O. I go south fo' the winter suh.

We had winds up to 35 knots tonight, but this ship didn't seem to roll much til after I left the watch. I guess the old bathtub is pretty stable after all.

1 February

(DC 3 landed in Little America)

Well bless my twinkling toes if another month hasn't rolled around. All I can say though is the little items at the top saying 333 days to come (the number of days left in the year) is rather disheartening.

The Little America base will close up on March 1st and the boys are hoping that we leave with them. I don't particularly care when we leave, but I'd rather that we didn't get back til after May 1st. Even then I'd like to hold off on a leave til the middle of June or so, so I could go to the graduation dance.

We had the same type of fog with us today that hampered our rescue operations a month ago.

The snow got so deep on the ship that I made a snowman on the catwalk. "So deep" in the previous statement doesn't mean anything like how much we get at home.

2 February

All day fog enclosed us. I sure hope that we haven't a certain number of flights to get off before the ship starts back. If we don't get any better weather than we've been having we'd be here til next Christmas. I got a big kick out of something I almost did during the watch. By mistake when I was coding up a weather message, I put the temperature where the present weather number should be. When it was decoded it read that we were having rows of sandstorms. I rushed over to the radio and corrected it just before they sent it out.

The barometric pressure got so low that on the barograph the pen arm ran off the bottom of the graph (*trace*). I reckon that it means we're in for a blow.

3 February

(No sign of ye olde stomach looping)
The so-called blow came and the waves really set the ship to rolling. They had to latch down all of the tables and what not, so we wouldn't be eating off someone else's plate at chow.

We broke 3 balloons sending up the Raysonde *(last night it was two, but when we finally did get it off, a down draft put the balloon right in the water)*. The instrument went under and for obvious reasons it sent 100% humidity. Later it came in good. The first had an instrument on it and it banged into two life boats causing the temperature and humidity to get knocked out. The fog that we still have is bad enough to put London to shame.

Oh yeah, I beat the chief and Le Grande in two games of hearts. (I *lost one by a point, too*).

4 February

(Been in 11 months today)

Tis a tough life I lead. Lately I've had twelve off twelve on, eighteen off four on, twelve off. Yes, a rugged life. This and the fact that I'm not getting up to eat is really making me pleasingly plump and I never felt much better in my life.

The chief spent a couple of nights writing a poem about this ship and trip and they published it in the daily "Pine Knot." It really tickled everyone with a sense of humor.

The Raysonde bounced off the smoke stack last night. The chief and I spent the evening playing Casino and 500 Rummy *(that's what I do when I work, I mean when I'm not eating)*.
Dumped 22 c soup (cp). (Translation: dumped 22 cans of the captain's soup in a side room for the guys.)

<u>5 February</u>

For the next couple of days I'll *(and everyone on the ship with me)* be watching the progress of the Brownson towards us. They are traveling ¼ the way around the world to bring us MAIL. The Philippine Sea brought it down when it carried Admiral Byrd to the S.P. (South Pole). They left early in January so the mail will be quite old. Maybe I'll get one little one out the 460 lbs reported to be on her.

Up again for GQ. (General Quarters means anything from a routine check to go to battle stations).

I looked up that Bob Benjamin from Watertown, finally. I was very disappointed as he told me that ever since he got in the Navy Waterville was being called Watertown. Tough.

The radio chief, our chief, LaGrande and yours truly polished off a heart game (*luckily I took the bows*).

6 February

The Brownson is being delayed about twelve hours while she is being refueled by the Canisteo. I guess we can stand waiting for a while longer.

I'm going to kinda hate to go home. Compared to the way I looked a year ago I'm almost bald. It's tough but I reckon I'll get used to the idea like everything else.

Started something new at the office. We have to start keeping logs on the sea and swell. (*It was supposed to be done from the start, but I guess the officers didn't read the operation plan until just lately so they just told us*). We have to stand outside with a stopwatch and time the length it takes for one swell to go by.

Lost at hearts and rummy, at least I was middle man both times.

7 February

Whew! That was close. We just got off watch before we got a flight out. It really is a lot of extra work when they are flying. (Dick is a weather guy, remember, so he had to supply wind velocity, direction barometric pressure, etc., settings).

I saw the moon for the first time in weeks. It looks just the same.

Also, for the first time in days the sky cleared up beautifully (*the reason for the flight*); the sun was a blinding glare to our unaccustomed eyes. It's a good chance for the other watch to get a record pibal sounding and beat the 17 minutes that we followed the balloon. I have a five buck bet that the other watch doesn't beat us for the highest Raysonde and pibal. So far we both hold one.

I also got a chance to take a few pictures. In my amateurish way, I always have the number ¾'s of the way out of the hole which will probably ruin some of the photos. (The box camera has a picture counter that appears to be out of synch).

Miller using theodolite

8 February

The weather cleared up good and we got a pibal to 17,000 ft. . The temperature got to 22 degrees which is really low for this trip. When I get home where it gets below 0 so continuously, I'll laugh at that, but I do know I got numb standing outside for a ½ hour. I don't really have the warm clothes (*at least I don't wear them at all*) to stay outside very long.

The Brownson rendevoused (*Oh, what sp.*) with us in the middle of the night. I could see them coming 15 or 20 miles away (there's daylight for most of the time). Everyone is happy because it means we will have a mail call today or tomorrow morning.

The place is really dotted with icebergs. I noticed one especially. It is a high affair that would look exactly like a carrier if it was dark out.

Collision mats (pancakes) for breakfast again. Looks like I hit the line more than once.

9 February

Aunt Lil's birthday. (Lillian McBride, lived to be about 93, a lovely lady).

Yippee! We got the mail. I did pretty good. 2 from Dad – 1- Mother, 1 - Art Alpert. 1-Thelma Camden, 1-Joan Cassidy, 1-Phil Phillipson, 1-Bill Wiley, 1-Elinor Holstein, 1-Anne Riley, 1-Mrs. Calkins, 1-Lucille Parsons, 2-Pat Orson, 1-Jean Oller, 1-Walt Barth.

Strangely enough those that I expected to hear from didn't get any news through. Ah well, it might be the mail system. News was up to the 20th of December. Dad has a '47 Olds. Bill Wiley and Bob Adams live near each other in Tokyo. Walt is in Japan. Junior Wiley is also in Japan. Phil Phillipson was in Greece soon to be homeward bound.

All in all I was quite satisfied with the number of letters and the fact that there was no bad news.

Walt sent a couple of pictures of Joy taken in Oklahoma (*twarn't bad*).

<u>10 February</u>

Boy oh boy, Santa came late (but he was sure welcome with his southern drawl) this year. When I awaken I found mucho letters under my sack. I didn't know they hadn't sorted them all yesterday. This time they were from 1-Bill, 1-Uncle Fred, 1-Dad, 1-Jean A., 1-Charlotte, 1-Alice, 1-Ed, 1-Stan, and finally another from Phil. Of all the letters that I received, the one that Phil mailed on the 23rd of December was the latest. Oh yes, I also got one from the "WDTimes" (Watertown Daily Times).

I really got a swell one from Uncle Fred and he hopes to make up for the times that we haven't met, by a get together in NY.

Phil is back in the states in R.I. He made a statement that I took to mean that he may be going up north. I'm going to apply for his ship because I think I'm going too.

I got me a little publicity in the paper (Watertown Daily Times). I didn't know that Bob Wells was on the Yancy. (The Yancy was on the same expedition with us).

I'm still way behind in receiving letters. The chief got one for the 3rd of January.

<u>11 February</u>

Well, what do you know, I managed to secure a little early for a change.

From now on my life will be a complete, confused, mess. My watch fell off my wrist as I was going up a ladder and the damn thing insisted on bouncing on every step on the way down. It is now in the category of those watches that are right only twice a day.

The Raconde went bounding along the water again and this time it conked out.

We are now approaching Margurette Bay where we will try to get some flight operations in progress. The Brownson will be there too. There might be some people sent ashore for the heck of it, but I'll never go, darn it.

12 February

I got another surprise today when I was handed a letter from Bob Adams. It was one of a few that had been pigeon holed. He corroborated Bill's story that the two of them were seeing each other quite a bit in Tokyo.

Today we saw something that I almost had forgotten existed. Yup. We saw land. It wasn't much, just a volcanic island but we could see dark spots under the snow-covered mountains.

About a month ago, aerology was handed the job of furnishing a compartment cleaner for the V division. Pi (Pipenbrink) took the first month and this noon I started taking charge of it for the second month. It's a humble job but it isn't hard and I have more free time that on my 12 hour watch.

The destroyer Brownson making a port turn

13 February

Over 35 knots of wind this morning. We picked up the Brownson and the thing is kicking and pitching like a bronco.

It was another uneventful day. I got back in my old form by chipping paint off the deck. We're making passages down to the metal then we will paint outside of them. I went to the educational office and got two books. One was on solid geometry and the other was a self-teacher on plain trigonometry. I don't know if I'll ever get the urge to study but if I do, they'll be handy.

I laid down at 1130 and fell asleep. I didn't wake up until 1400 which is an hour after turn to. (When you go to work).

The sea is so rough that they won't let anyone topside except the watches and even they have a rope about them.

14 February

Another emergency presented itself today. Commodore Duftex was being transferred from the Brownson to us by a breeches chair. (Put two ropes between a pulley, and a chair is hooked to the two ropes, fixed on one, rolling on the other. The guy sits in the chair and you pull the ropes in like a clothesline. You transport him form one ship to another). The two ships leaned in opposite directions and the line snapped. He was hit by a pulley and dropped into the icy Antarctic waters. Due to wonderful ship handling, the Brownson was able to pick him up within ten minutes. He isn't too bad off after his second swim (*the other when the helicopter crashed*).

We had field day in the morning and I worked quite hard. The afternoon inspection was cancelled because we were refueling the Brownson. Inasmuch as the compartment was clean, I took the afternoon off. I spent most of it signaling semaphore to Caldwell on the Brownson. That ship really takes a beating. He claims they had a 42° roll during the storm the other day.

There is talk that we may go to Montevideo in Uruguay on the way back north.

15 February

Worked a couple of hours in the A.M. and took the rest of the day off.

We had the first ship's smoker last night and we hope to have them every Saturday night from now on. It consisted of 8 boxing matches in the hanger deck. The equivalent of a T.M. kept us in stitches between bouts by telling jokes. Most of the matches drew blood. After, we went to the mess hall and put down ham sandwiches.

During the noon hour the Capt. came off the P.A. system and talked to us about what has been accomplished and what we were to do next. We're on our way to meet the Canisteo and from there we will go around the Palmer Peninsula to search for better flying weather. The Northwind and the Yancy are going to take the Merrick to Wellington, N.Z. to make repairs.

16 February

Oh yes when the Capt. talked to us yesterday he also said we were going to leave in a couple of weeks. Just a minor detail (sarcasm). I was hoping that we wouldn't get back until May, but I guess it will be sooner. The reason that I wanted May was because there would be a chance to get my rate. As I said before, I passed my test. If I don't get it in May, I'll have to wait 3 or 6 months. This peace time Navy is tough unless you're assigned permanently.

I had the day off and for the first time in a long time, I found myself in church.

I played volley ball all afternoon and had loads of fun. I got real stiff and sore so I reckon I'm not in condition. *(Sore, mainly because I fell flat on my back on my knife).*

17 February

Another easy day. With all the sleep that I'm getting it's no wonder I'm feeling good. It was a swell day out and one could go outside with just a sweater on and still feel comfortable.

The Canisteo is on our port beam and the Brownson is off our starboard. As far as I can remember, it's the first time we've all been together since we separated upon entering the operating area.

The other fellows say the chow is terrible – I love it and I almost think I have had it better in the Navy. I have to cut down to 2 meals a day so I won't get heavy (*as soon as I can't see my ribs very good I stop eating*).

I read "The Postman Always Rings Twice." Purdy good. If I ever get the energy to go the library I guess I could find some good books.

18 February

I went to the movie for the first time since Friday. Jinny Simms had the boys howling in "Shady Lady."

At 1600 sharp when they pipe "Sweepers, man your brooms." Miller, *(he has to be different)* drops his and heads for the hangar. There's a volley ball game commencing where a moment before there were engines roaring and all kinds of hubbub that usually takes place during the working day. Today the enlisted men beat the officers.

They had the skill but we had the youth and desire to beat them.

The water was just about as rough as we've had it so far. They have hooks in all of the showers and you really have to hold on. Needless to say things happen in the chow hall that keep us laughing.

19 February

Our Lenten season began today but I won't be going to our usual Friday night services. I am really surprised at the number of fellows who not only don't know what Lent is for but haven't even heard of it. This year I intended to give up candy, but my lack of foresight caught me with ¾ of a box of Hershey bars in my locker. For the last reason I decided to give up ice cream. I usually have a couple of cups of it a day so I'll really miss it.

Six of us beat six officers in volley ball after work. I get a big kick out of it because it's the first chance I've had to use a little energy since I left.

20 February

Well bless my buttons, if I didn't draw some money today *($10)*. It's the first time since the payday before we left the states. I wound up spending $23 at the ship's store.

We had a general quarters drill today. As usual we heard about it ahead of time and I knocked off work *(so called)* an hour ahead of time in order to be ready.

We had our usual game with the officers etc. We trounced them 21-6 in the first. We followed that by 21-4 victory over the chiefs. The next game the officers took us over the hurdles 20-22.

We also had a locker inspection during which Lt. Gayelle complimented me on mine. Why, I don't know.

21 February

A number of things occurred.

Firstly, I had to work pretty hard in the morning getting things ready for inspection. After the field day that I held, it was cancelled because we were being refueled by the Canisteo *(I haven't been to the office in so long I don't even know where we are)*.

An Antarctic bird of some sort landed on the helicopter and one of the fellows grabbed it. They showed it to the Capt. and he had it sent over to a scientist aboard the Canisteo.

An unusual thing happened toward suppertime. On the horizon a ship was seen with guns firing and all the lookouts were reporting it. Later we heard from the Brownson that they had neglected to tell us that they were test firing their guns.

We had our usual games of VB (volley ball) in which we defeated the officers and chiefs.

I'm getting to be a chow hound again which I thought I had conquered. Four or five meals a day besides about four candy bars ought to help my indigestion.

22 February

Last night we finished the evening off with a box of crackers and a pound of butter while tonight found us gorging ourselves with hot dogs and apple pie *(on the rough)*.

My total work for the day consisted of sweeping the compartment twice. The rest of the day I fluffed off.

Our usual Saturday night smoker was pretty good. We had comedy, singing, boxing and wrestling *(followed by refreshments)*.

Our trek around the peninsula *(Palmer)* seems to have been in vain. Ice extends for hundreds of miles from the continent making it impractical to try and get off exploring flights. This section of the continent is explained on maps by one big word, Unexplored. We are getting quite far east now and if we went straight north we would just about hit Capetown, South Africa.

23 February

Sundays we have holiday routines so all I did was sweep down a couple of times. Today we skirted the thickest ice pack that we have come in contact with so far. Natch, it's such thick ice that it keeps us from moving closer to land.

1000 (ten hundred) found me in church this morning. The Chaplain gives a fair sermon but it sounds like he thinks he's talking to a bunch of dopes. It's the first Sunday in Lent. According to plan we are to be back in Norfolk the second of April. If we manage to get a leave right away, I may get home for Easter. I kinda hope so being that I missed Christmas.

I stood a two hour watch up on the boat deck crane last night. It was quite cold but I had enough foul weather gear on to be comfortable (*the fact that I got $3 for standing the watch was alright too*).

24 February

For a change they almost insisted that I do a little work. A couple of weeks ago we chipped passages in the deck. Today we buffed, emery papered and steel wooled those parts until they got real shiny.

Above is the artist's conception of the three-pronged land and sea novel expedition which uncovered more of Antarctica than all former expeditions put together. The continent irregularly draped around the South Pole covers six million square miles, much of it still unseen.

33

I got a map of the Antarctic and when I get time I'm going to plot our course on it (note the back cover of the book, which is a section of the plotted course on a map done by the author). It won't be impressive, but at least it will help me remember where we were.

We're starting a volley ball tournament. The first set (*four games*) was played. At twenty-four-hundred they are setting the clocks ahead two hours, which means we're losing two hours sleep.

I broke out my canoe trip pictures and even though the fellows were insistent on seeing pictures of girls I was more insistent on explaining in gruesome details all about the trip. Then I showed them, midst various comments, da gals.

<u>25 February</u>

We spent the day on the deck again. I'm literally earning the right be called a Swabbie.

It was a beautiful day so I took almost a whole roll of film. (At most you get 12 for the box camera.) I put part of my furs on for the occasion. I'll have to send a picture to Thelma.

From what I hear, all of the other ships in the central and western groups have started back to the states. (*maybe a rumor*)

We asked (*the captain asked*) permission to return, because we're too far from the continent to do any operating. Permission refused.   Now we are proceeding to the 0° meridian. (*That's the Greenwich that passed directly through England*). When we get there we'll probably turn around and go back.

I bought a new pair of shoes and I intend to work on them for a few hours getting them ready for captain's inspection on the way to Rio. (You want new shoes to shine, so you polish them, shine them, polish them, spit on them, put several layers of polish on them.)

The boys are a little P.O.'d because I took laundry tonight instead of tomorrow A.M.

<u>26 February</u>

I reckon that even down here we aren't completely obscured from civilization. Today we made, or rather encountered, several ships. We saw them at a distance and increased our speed to get nearer. The other ships ran but we overhauled them and distinguished them as Russian whalers. There were 2 mother ships, so to speak, and each had whale chasers out. We proceeded on our way after coming within 30 yd. of them.

Finally finished the deck.

My division is bunked right over the screws (propellers). The Pine Island is a twin screw job and right now something is wrong with one. It's causing the ship to vibrate here in the fantail and I believe it may cut down our speed on our return voyage.

I just heard that we can take another 3rd class test March 20. I still won't have my time in, but I might as well take the test.

<u>27 February</u>

Lately we've been doing something I like. Everyday we have a drill of some type at 1530. The last 3 days it's been fire, G.Q. (general quarters), and abandon ship. It makes the working day seem short (*it's easy enough as it is*).

I've been eating like a pig as of late (*that includes about 4 bars of candy a day*). And tonight I paid for some of it. I got a wicked stomach that bothered me no end. I reckon that

I had better control myself (*I did have four bowls of peaches for supper*).

Today I was a little lucky and I beat Adam MM 1/c in two games of chess. (*You have to ruin your eyes to try to see the men*).

My whole afternoon was fluffed off cleaning my swabs out. I just tied them to a line and dragged them off the fantail (*had my picture taken by a fellow, a big berg in the background*).

We should cross the zero meridian tonight. I wish it were the 180th so I could get a golden dragon card.

I must be cracking up because I spent about three hours polishing my new shoes. (*author has drawn a picture depicting a size 13 shiny shoe*).

I watched LeGrande playing poker in C Division. He lost 45 dollars as I watched so I left to change his luck.

All of the fellows are begging for maps of the Antarctic like mine.

28 February

They finished the month off with a rigid inspection of my compartment (*fair*).

Today we were supposed to start back to the states, but everything is fouled up. Instead of going north we headed due south in order to get nearer the coast to continue operations. The captain talked to us and said that we had to get a couple more hops (planes taking photographs for mapping purposes) in before we leave.

Rumors are flying. We are now supposed to go to the west coast in place of the Currituck. If so I won't get a leave. That would also probably cut out our visit to Rio.

Last night at 2030 we crossed the 0° meridian and the Antarctic Circle at the same time. Not many ships have done that. We get a card for rounding the horn (*this way – west to east- instead of this way – east to west*).(Most explores would round it going east to west).

V-3 beat V-2 in volley ball yesterday. They claim they were robbed.

I didn't eat any meals today.

Saw "Easy to Look At" at the movies.

1 March

Ah yes, March came in like a lamb down here (*it probably marked the end of the skating season back home*). It was cold but sunny and for that reason we got the well known call of "FLIGHT QUARTERS". We thought that if we got in these two flights we would be able to start back, so everyone worked with a will. In a zoom of jet the planes took off only to return about three hours later with the news that they ran into bad weather over the continent (*about 40 m away*). I got a few pictures and I sure hope they come out.

We had our Saturday night smoker of 8 fights and a few numbers by the ship's band. Afterwards they served cake and ice cream. It sure tore my heart out not to be able to eat that free ice cream (*remember, I gave it up for Lent*). I ended up by trading the ice cream for more cake.

If the article I have pasted at the top doesn't stay, it just says that the central fleet is starting homeward (*I hope we don't run out of food before they let us go back north*).

2 March

They had flight quarters again last night but the weather moved in and stopped the operation. I didn't even get up. In fact I slept right through til 1215 (*got up for breakfast*) Sunday afternoon (*14 hr.*).. I love weekends now that I'm a department cleaner. Since 1300 Fri., all I have done is swept down once on Saturday. I intended to go to church but I just didn't wake up.

I worked on my Antarctic map and almost brought it up to date as far as Feb is concerned.

I skipped noon chow, the best meal of the week, because I knew I wouldn't have the willpower to resist the ice cream they had for dessert. Their large store of food begins to lack in a few places. The oranges ran out last week and I think we finished up the apples this morning.

Saw the Dr. Gilispie picture "Three Men in White." The way Van Johnson turned down the advances of a beautiful blonde drove the fellows wild.

Part Four: Leaving Little America

3 March

The Capt spoke to us again about 0700 this morning saying that the commander of CTG68.3 has declared our flight operations at an end. We are now withdrawing from the Antarctic. Boy, needless to say that brought forth a cheer from hundreds of tired fellows that resounded throughout the vessel.

RIO HERE WE COME – actually we headed north last evening, but we got the official word today. The ship's top speed is about 14 knots now (*bad screw*). One of the first things that I do will be to get me a big tall glass of milk. The other fellows say I'm crazy, but I miss it.

We beat V-2 in volleyball last evening so that makes 2 won and 1 loss.

We had a general quarters drill in the afternoon.

GROUPS LEAVING LITTLE AMERICA

Fast-Freezing Ice Conditions in Bay of Whales Causing Concern.

By LEE VAN ATTA

On Board the U. S. S. Mount Olympus, Feb. 24.—The final meal at historic Little America was to be served Sunday noon, after which all equipment being left behind will be stored underground and personnel loaded aboard the icebreaker Burton Island for evacuation.

Rear Admiral Richard E. Byrd and Richard H. Cruzen radioed shortly before noon antarctic time Sunday that Little America would definitely be abandoned "within twelve hours."

Captain R. S. Quackenbush declared that both admirals were particularly concerned over fast-freezing ice conditions in the Bay of Whales.

Also causing the expedition's leaders some anxiety were disturbing reports that the Great Ross sea ice pack is consolidating and steadily spreading south.

Nearly 200 air operations men, headed by Byrd, will be brought out on the anticipated three-day dash through the ice.

At the same time Byrd and Cruzen made their decision to cancel operations of the central group, Captain Charles Bond's western task group radioed it too had been forced to turn back homeward after having penetrated more than half way around the Antarctic continent.

Reports from the U. S. S. Currituck, western flagship, said that warnings of a harsh Antarctic winter are visible everywhere, and that flying weather was steadily deteriorating.

The task group reversed course last night. The Currituck, accompanied by the destroyers Henderson, Opler, and Cacapon, headed for Sydney, Australia, by way of the Balleny Islands. From Sydney the group will leave for the States.

85

I finished the evening with a freezing session with R. Rogers in "Light of Old Santé Fe."

4 March

Bang, at 0100 we were rolled to the deck to the tune of "fire fire FIRE." Half dressed as I was I was running around on the flight deck and weather decks to get to my fire station. The fire was in the carpenter shop and was soon extinguished.

Happy Anniversary, Dick. Yup, you've been in a year today and I'll bet you don't feel 365 days older. Of course you are fatter and balder, but keep your chins up and you'll be out in a year. I wouldn't take a discharge now if I could get one. Too far to swim.

I read where all of my boys who were drafted will be out by June 1st. The unlucky devils think they are getting a good deal getting out of service. I'm thinking of re-enlisting.

I shaved off my three month's moustache. It was beginning to get in my food when the ends curled up (*I look about 19 with it off*).

5 March

2524 miles to Rio at 1200.

Just my usual fluff off day, I guess. We got paid again *($10)* but I owed it to LeGrande.

The afternoon I took off to write letters in the balloon shack. They were my first attempt in quite a while but it didn't matter how bad they were because I lost them. *(Later in the evening after I had rewritten the letters, I found the notebook with them in it.)*

All of the boys are working like mad on their shoes in preparation for inspection Saturday. The main discussion is whether it will be in blues or whites.

I decided to inform the folks that I was coming *(or going)* home instead of trying to surprise them.

We are still seeing icebergs.

6 March

I was busy most of the day sorting clothes. It takes several hours to do 6 big bags of them.

We beat the C division in volleyball so that puts us right up among the leaders in the tournament.

For a 9 ½ lb. baby, I guess it was worth three boxes of cigars. No, not mine you dope. Hartswick, in our division *(BM2)*, got the good word today by telegram and he was very generous. The cigars caused almost as many casualties as the first few days of the cruise. (Everybody got sick). "Help someone pull me back from the rail". No, I learned my lesson before and I don't indulge in them.

The bad news came today. We are to go to Rio for a few days, proceed to the Panama Canal and from there whiz off to San Diego. I saw the dispatch so I know it's official. There are a lot of sad faces aboard but I reckon I am still young enough to want to see the world.

7 March

For a change I worked hard all morning on field day. I really got mad inside when I saw how little cooperation I got from the fellows. They all had their clothes lying all over. I hated to do it, but I just picked it all up and gave it the deep 6. One would really be surprised at the amount of gear that goes over the side. I wish I could have it all home. We got a few complaints during inspection but none were my fault.

We've run into the worst weather of the trip. I was just up at the office and we had a true wind of 52 knots and an apparent wind of 61 knots. We can really lean into it. We have a very heavy sea but luckily we're heading into it *(9 kts speed is reduced to 5 ½ by the sea)*. The Capt. just said that we will be in the states about April 16th. We'll hit San Diego the 16th of April instead of Norfolk the 2nd of April. Tough for us easterners.

8 March

I think the boys said the wind hit 58 true, 62 apparent. I labeled all of my pictures that I brought with me. Oh what a racket I have. Now they send two guys down in the morning to help me sweep up (*about time, too*) which is about the only thing I do.

We were supposed to provision the Brownson which is down to about its last piece of hard tack, but the sea was too rough. I took the afternoon off as usual and took a few pictures. I think I'd better go easy on film in case we can't get it at Rio.

The Saturday night smoker featured 3 knockouts and a T.K.O. out of 8 matches. They had to carry one guy out. All the hamburgs we wanted were at our disposal after the fights. I've been eating too much candy lately, so I'm going to stop giving up ice cream for lent and switch to candy. I think we saw about our last iceberg today.

Even the Capt. admitted that we were living on borrowed time with all this fog and icebergs that we have to put up with as it is the ice that has ruined one screw and in one spot it ruined our hull. It was mostly done when we had to make knots in the fog. What bothered me more was

having all of these fumes from the high (*100*) octane gas. (*The explosives were the least of our worries.*)

9 March

I found myself in church again.

V-3 beat H division in volleyball so that makes a 3 way tie for 1st.

I did a couple hours work remaking my Antarctic map. I lent the 1st one to so many fellows that it got all fouled up.

We saw the movie "Keys of the Kingdom" with Gregory Peck and it was the best we've had in a long time.

Another berg was seen after all.

I filled up on luscious ham during the noon meal, but we ate _ _ i _ the rest of the meals.

The weather was swell even though it was a bit snappy.

10 March

After going the whole cruise practically without any plane trouble, the Currituck finally lost one on her return trip. They had apparent winds up to 92 knots that tore one of her planes loose and gave it the deep 6.

As usual I didn't do anything but clean the scuttlebutt and empty the trashcan. Boy, am I getting lazy.

V-3 won volleyball again so we are still in the running.

There are a lot of rumors flying around that those of us that are under the flag are getting off in Panama. We would get on the Currituck (*another sea plane tender*) and report in at Philadelphia.

A comb, a comb, my kingdom for a comb. I lost my only 2 combs today and can't get anymore. There is a drastic shortage of them aboard.

<u>11 March</u>

We re-provisioned the Brownson today but I didn't get any pictures. They had an all hands working party so I went in the balloon shack to fluff off. (*They had more than was needed anyway*)

The sun was out bright as gold and it seemed strange to see the fellows without foul weather gear on. Big albatrosses were gliding about the ship today so that indicated good luck in the future.

Hit the balloon shack again from 3 to 7. Missed chow as a result but who cares.

Right after we got out of the movies and I walked across the flight deck, I noticed the moon was out almost full. It was really shining away and it was hard to believe that the folks back home were gazing at the same scene.

12 March

Should be off from compartmental cleaning. I had four weeks of it today and they decided to give me another week of it. The other fellows (*Pi + Simp*) will have had the same so it doesn't bother me any. I'm not kidding when I say that I don't work 3 hrs a day (except *Wed & Fri am*).

I find it awfully hard to believe the weather has changed so much. I don't know what the temperature has risen to but I've been sweating all day. It's just like changing from winter to summer without the gradual change that spring brings.

I decided to start studying for my 3rd class test (*should have begun a long time ago*) that we get soon. As usual I still haven't my time in, but I'll take it for practice. Studied in the balloon shack til after taps. (*alright, so I started 10 minutes before taps*).

13 March

I'm afraid that I was a busy little seaman today. I scrubbed hoses, steel wooled decks, swabbed and oiled them, etc. I didn't mind it so bad after I found out that there won't be any inspection tomorrow. We're going to have to clean up the ship.

It was a big event with the loud speaker boomed that "Sun bathing will be allowed from 1130 to 1300." You should have seen the fellows scramble when the time came. The only disappointment seemed in the fact that you had to wear at least skivvy shorts. The temp. got to be in the seventies and the skins that had been protected by foul weather gear for months became red quickly.

I went to the movies last night instead of studying as I intended (*just no willpower*).

I broke out the blue trunks I bought from Pelman in 1945 (Pelman ran the boy's & men's shop in Watertown, NY).

14 March

It was another roaster so at noon hour we all headed for the flight deck. We look like a bunch of Hollywood stars wearing our sunglasses. (*They were issued us*)

I took it easy most of the day; I spent most of my time trying to dodge the working party that was sent over the side to clean the ship.

We refueled the Brownson most of the morning and I saw Caldwell as bright as life on her. I hope to see him on liberty in Rio.

We (*V-3*) were supposed to have a couple playoff games with H division for championship of the "A" league. The officers decided they wanted to play so we stood in the background. C'est la guerre.

All of the boys in aerology got a few pictures apiece, courtesy of photographers. They're a good thing to have in case my snapshots don't come out.

<u>15 March</u>

The boys were glad when they cancelled the Captains inspection. Everyone hated to dirty a clean set of whites.

We saw some shark swimming around the fantail yesterday and some of the boys announced their intention of catching him.

Our usual holiday routine for Sat. pm was cancelled in order to clean the sides of the ship. (*I fluffed off all day per usual*).

We had the playoff for the volleyball tournament and "The News Is Not Good Tonight." We lost the first game, won the second and were defeated in the third by a score of 21-18. I still think we have the better team, but it was fun all around.

We're only a couple hundred miles from Rio.

<u>16 March</u>

Remember my talking about that shark yesterday? Well today they got him. I was up there when they pulled him on deck and he chased us all around with his thrashing. He finally got himself tangled up in the line and plane cables. I got a couple of bad pictures of him (*later five more were caught*).

In the afternoon I just laid in the sun and played volleyball. I received a pretty good sunburn for it all. A few of us got up a game against the officers and came out on the large end of the score.

Saw a pretty good movie with Pat O'Brien.

Bearman PHOM 3/c gave me some pictures taken on the trip. I may get to have quite a few yet.

It was the kind of day that they advertise in the recruiting office.

17 March

As usual (*that expression is getting usual in itself*) the other's sweated while Dicky took it easy. I wrote a few letters to mail in Rio and played cards.

Capt's inspection went off OK and they succeeded in making us all dirty a set of whites. At the inspection they made a number of presentations of letters of commendations for various services.

They saw the lights of Rio and many claim that they saw land itself. Knowing how bad my eyes are, I didn't even try.

I found out that it cost a small fortune to send a telegram from Rio so I guess I'll have to let a letter suffice.

Miller toasting a successful trip to Rio de Janeiro

I would say that it was rather a big day. We entered Rio harbor about 0800 and it was indescribably beautiful. The modern building at Copacabana contrasted with old forts and shrines. Outlined against the sky were numerous mountains, the most famous being Sugarloaf (*and the breathtaking cable car ride to its peak where there is a nice restaurant*). And nearby, a larger MT with a 150' statue of Christ on its summit soaring into the sky.

In the traditional Pine Island style the liberty party was detained 2 ½ hours so we didn't hit the beach until 1545. What I mean is that they hit it as only sailors who have been over 3 months without, could.

We hopped a taxi and I finally convinced him that we wanted to go to Copacabana Beach and not "Casa De Gattos" (not the cat house). We first had a steak barbecue. It was an open restaurant where they cooked the meat on sticks over an open fire and it was really quite delicious. Following that we went sightseeing.

19 March

Liberty up at 0100. After 4 hours sleep I ate and ran up to the starboard gangway. I had to stand a watch as the commodore's orderly (*slave*). I waited up there until about 0930 when he decided to come aboard. He looked OK but I think he had a hard liberty because the doctor went up to his cabin (*T.G.H.P.I.*).

They sure had good news in the way of mail. I received 8 letters in the AM and 12 came to my open arms in the afternoon. I stayed up til 2330 answering them. There were 2 from Art, 3 from Phil, 1 from Kitty Schultz, 1 from Joan Cassidy, 1 from Mrs. Adams, 1 from Ed, 1 from Mother, 1 from Mel Pollack, 2 from Aud, and I guess the rest from Dad.

We had some Brazilian officers aboard but I don't think they look as sharp as ours.

20 March

Worked a little in the AM getting stores ready for the Brownson.

At 1030, I got the word from the executive officer that I had to be present as a guest of the commandant of the 1st

Naval District. There were 20 of us who had to go. It was to be a trip up to Corcavado MT (sp) to see the statue of Christ. An avalanche fell across the tramway tracks so the trip was cancelled. Instead we took a 2 hr. trip of Rio and the outskirts by bus. I was impressed by how beautiful so many of the houses were built. They were much nicer than in the US.

Simpson, myself, Caldwell, Brown and Mando put down a swell steak dinner. We picked up Chief at the restaurant and took the cable ride to the top of Sugarloaf Mt. It was truly beautiful to see the lights of the city, the harbor and to gasp as the car rose in the air hundreds of feet above the ground. I would like to go up again to see how it looks in the daytime. After that we went to a large USO dance which was a good deal better than any I've ever been to before. It was in the spacious dining hall of the Automotive Bureau of Brazil. There were 150 girls and an equal number of sailors which is strange in itself. The dance was held especially for the ships in our task group. I danced with 2 girls who had actually been through Watertown and had heard of it.

I bought a tray and a wallet for souvenirs.

21 March

Liberty, up at 0100. A little groggy when I woke up but as the day progressed I wasn't so tired. I found that I was still on compartment cleaning so I straightened the place up a little for field day. I didn't work as hard as I do when inspection is coming up. I had the Commodore's orderly watch in the PM. The Capt. and the Commodore had a big party in their state room with about 40 people. There were a lot of Brazilian officers and a number of women.

I had to spend most of my spare time trying to keep a set of whites clean all the time.

I got a letter from Phil. He's really on the ball. It makes 4 letters in 3 days that I've received.

22 March

I'm afraid that we fouled up a little in this port. Late night there were riots and I understand that a Brownson sailor was killed. A number of our fellows were shot at. It's for the above reason that we only got liberty from 1300 to 1800 in order not to be out after dark. Jake LeGrande AerM 1/c and I went ashore and got a big meal. We then went to Copacabana so Jake could telegram his wife. I sent another just for the hell of it. (*I hope it isn't taken wrong*).

I fouled up a couple of pictures that I took by not turning the film.

So now I'm back on the ship for a couple weeks. "Next stop, Panama. All out!"

Quelle belle fille. Ugh.

23 March

Most of the fellows got to go ashore early to go to church but inasmuch as I had the duty I went to church aboard. The guys left church early and resumed the things that sailors usually do ashore. I must say that when they were hauled aboard they were in much better condition than our section was. (*Myself and a couple of others excluded*).

I hit the rack most of the afternoon. I had the Commodore's orderly watch from 6 to 10, however I thought he was ashore so I went to the movies. (*Later it turned out that he sneaked aboard and hit the rack*). I went up to the crow's nest and got one last look at the lights of Rio. For a few minutes I was content to be a sailor.

24 March

Well, I finally got off compartment cleaning. Pi took over again and the place is beginning to be livable again. As I said before, I never did much work on it.

We set the special sea detail and pulled out of Rio Harbor at 1000. It was pretty even between the fellows who liked the place and those who were glad to go.

I puttered around all afternoon and I finally took the 1800 to 2100 watch at the office. That consisted of trying to remember some card tricks I learned at the Gordon's house and for reading a few spicy chapters of the Dutchess Hotspur. All in all you can see that it was a mighty tough watch. (*What little tan I had is peeling off*)

Leaving Rio for Panama

Sugarloaf Mt. in the background

25 March

Had to work a bit longer than usual today because we picked up 93 maps in Rio that we have to copy before we get to Panama. It takes me a couple of hours to do one, so it's quite a task.

My chance to lay in the sun was ruined by heavy rain showers. Down here in the tropics they are scattered throughout the day usually with a hot sun breaking through after they pass.

We can't read during working hours so I put the Duchess Hotspur inside a meteorology book and continued reading.

Saw an old picture with G. Cooper and Jean Arthur, "Mr. Deeds Goes to Town."

<u>26 March</u>

Had the 6 to 12 watch in the A.M.

It was the most beautiful day we had so far and I couldn't help but take advantage of it by laying in the sun awhile. The temperature reached 90° which is higher than we usually get during the summer at home.

I crapped out in the balloon shack til 1600 and then took in a cool breeze by sitting on the flight deck. After supper I climbed in my rack til 2330 when I got up to go on watch.

They're easing up a little as far as the *(c.s)* goes. They now let us take off our shirts and wear just the skivi tops *(etc.)*

We're doing better speed than we planned so we ought to get to Panama a day or so early.

<u>27 March</u>

I got to sleep in all day because I worked during the night, however, due to the heat I had to be mostly satisfied with daydreaming. It was raining so I couldn't take my usual few minutes in the sun.

One of these days I'll have to wrap up the souvenirs I got in Rio because I noticed they are getting a little bumped up in my locker. I hear we'll have to open our seabags for customs inspection when we hit the states to see that we haven't over $100 worth of foreign goods.

After my 6-9:30 watch I sat on the deck in the cool breezes shooting the breeze with the fellows and gazing at the moon. Lost 25c to ensign Huscke when he held his arms out straight for 5 minutes.

28 March

I just happened to remember. In case anyone happens to read this thing, I just want to confirm something. In South America people do walk around with big bundles on their heads. They have a remarkable sense of balance and are able to sport large sacks, baskets, etc. with ease.

We (*Jake and I*) finished our quota of maps so now we go back on our regular watch schedule.

I got a little volley ball practice as we warmed up the champs of the "A" league for their forthcoming match with the "B" league. We beat them in a couple fast games.

Another day of 90 degrees.

We are scheduled to arrive in Panama on Easter day April 6th, instead of the 9th.

<u>29 March</u>

Had the morning watch (6-12).

There was holiday routine in the P.M. as yours truly was going to spend a good deal of the time in the sun. Heavy rain showers put an end to my plans, so I settled for playing catch and refining (*not sure that is the word, but it will do!*) the championship volley ball game. They looked like they were getting ready to throw things at me so I rushed down right after and hit the rack.

We rounded the Bulge anyway, I mean the most easterly point of South America. Now we're headed 305 degrees.

I have the night watch from 9:30 to 7:30 A.M. during which I hope to get a little reading of Bob Hope's book, "I Never Left Home."

<u>30 March</u>

Dragged myself off the night watch all ready to sleep the day through. I decided to wake up and got to 930 church (*being Palm Sunday*). After that, at 1030, I came to conclusion that dinner was worth waiting up for (*all of the baked ham we wanted*). I laid in the sun for an hour. The weather was warm and a good sunburn was enjoyed by all.

It was too hot sleeping in the compartment so I went topside to rest. To make it short I spent the rest of the afternoon playing volleyball and hence I did sleep. Went on watch 6:00 to 9:30 P.M. and finally hit the rack for the first time (*except for two hours yesterday*) in 40 hours.

We crossed the equator at 5 o'clock this morning, but it was too dark to see it.

31 March

And another month has passed.

There was a call for a working party in the A.M. when I was free and in the course of dodging it, I saw the engine room for the first time. It's 2 or 3 decks below my sleeping quarters and it's the first time I've been down that far.

LeGrande's and my game of catch was cut short as he flipped the ball over the side. Sports for sports.

The fellows are finding it hard to believe that we will be back in the states in a little over two weeks. I'm even looking forward to the receiving ship where five of the aerographers are being transferred to the four winds (terminology that means it can go in any direction).

Panama is being reached the 7th instead of the 6th now (*navigator missed a little*).

1 April

Hummingbird's wings on toast were on the menu for this morning. Of course it was the officer's menu, but they didn't get it because it was April Fool's Day.

We had the A.M. watch, so after a little sunbathing, I looked for a nice place to crap out in preparation for the night watch. I found it in the form of an old, dirty mattress in a dark corner of the next compartment.

We saw "The Werewolf" at the movies and for a change I was glad we had the night watch because I don't think I could sleep after the movie anyway. Belay that last remark because I slept on the deck in the balloon shack from 3-6:30 in the morning.

We had the current with us so we picked up a few extra miles.

2 April

Got off watch at 630 and crapped out. In the afternoon when I was supposed to be sleeping they sent for me to go on a working party. LeGrande Aerm 1/c got mad at the idea and went to the officer to complain (*he was protecting me*). He couldn't sway him so instead of coming back and telling me I had to work, he went to work himself (he took my job). Believe me, 1/c petty officers don't have to haul 100 lb. sacks of flour around. "A friend in need- etc.."

I finished my Antarctic map late in the evening and now I'm going to try to get the signatures of everyone in the V-division. I also managed to dash off a couple letters to be mailed in Panama.

Tomorrow morning we're going within a few miles of Trinidad, but inasmuchas I'll be sleeping, I'll miss seeing it.

<u>3 April</u>

The A.M. found me sleeping contrasted to the afternoon when I was on a flour moving detail. Remember my talking of working on one early on the cruise? At that time we moved about 80,000 lbs down into one of the central magazines. We're now moving it back to where it came from.

Inasmuchas it's Holy Thursday (*Maundy*) I went to communion. It was a pretty good service. (*at least there were more guys there to make it seem like home church*) We have a little organ that one of the fellows plays that even makes the good singers (*ahem*) sound bad.

They had a pretty good old time movie with Jimmy Stewart. Remember "Mr. Smith Goes to Washington?"

<u>4 April</u>

11 months to go

Took over the flour sacks this A.M. (author drew picture of flour sack)

Polished up my seabag to get ready for the long journey from the P.I. to Currituck.

This afternoon I again found the hangar deck taking on a religious aspect. We had Good Friday services and the chaplain was pretty good again (didn't matter what religion you were, it was the same chaplain).

The division will soon have a corner on the baby market. Two more of the fellows became Papas for the first time and I again got my quota of cigars.

The last two days have been beautiful. I should say the nights, because looking at the full moon as we sit out on the gallery deck, the sky and the moon seem to enhance even *this* ship. We are now in the same time zone as at home, so now I can picture more accurately the things that are happening under that same moon.

5 April

I had the all night watch, which gave me the privilege of sleeping through captain's inspection. At the inspection they gave out citations for a bunch of minor things. At 1000 I got up for payday and this time I drew 22 twenties, 1 five and 3 ones. Yup. $448 which was all I had on the books came into my hands. I spent a good part of the day waiting in line to get 4 one hundred dollar money orders. *(The stubs are in the back of this book)*

I laid in the sun for a little over an hour and it will probably turn out to be my last chance til we hit the states. I had the 1800-2100 watch and even then I went to the movies during that.

We hit the canal zone tomorrow which will probably mean a couple hours of liberty. I'm not looking forward to it quite as much as last time.

6 April

Yup, today is Easter and we're all looking for Easter Eggs. The nearest thing to it that I found was a heel off a woman's shoe in the executive officer's room.

The Easter service was lacking as might be expected.

We tied up *(for the first time since last December)* at the air station pier at about 1400. Mail was waiting on the dock for us and about an hour later I was handed a letter from Phil. I thought that was darn good service.

I went ashore to prowl around at about 1700. Colón is better than Panama City although it too has a good many faults. We gorged ourself with chow and I followed it up with 2 banana splits. I bought a watch for Mother at the USO and I hope I didn't get robbed. All the shops had nice alligator goods but I didn't have enough talent to find out how cheap they would sell.

7 April

Ah, it was just four months ago today that we went through the Panama Canal on the way south. As we went through again today, I couldn't help but be glad we didn't have to do it all over again. The size of the locks still fascinated me but the amount of concrete that was used made me wonder that the undertaking was completed as fast as it was.

Since the Commodore wasn't aboard *(I was his orderly)* in the afternoon I washed clothes and wrote letters. I had

six letters and a newspaper to keep me entertained with news from home.

It took us from 9-4:30 pm to transit the canal which was a longer time than before. All the fellows were mad because they didn't get liberty until after 6 o'clock.

8 April

I managed to dodge all the working parties so when liberty call came I was raring to go. Jake LeGrande and I went ashore and the first thing we did was to have a swim at the Balboa Clubhouse. That was the same place I went swimming on my journey south only this time my mind was a little more at ease.

We had a big meal and headed for Panama City. We spent the usual amount of time shopping around and bargaining *(which I'm not so hot at)* with the shop keepers. Jake bought a ring watch and an automatic cigarette lighter. I found myself buying a cheap watch which I don't expect to keep good time but which might hold over until I get mine fixed.

We took in a couple of floor shows and headed back to the P.I. *(I had to be back at 2330)*

Party in Panama

9 April

As usual I sat around all morning reading magazines (*they have them only a few days late in Panama*).

At noon we got our check out cards and we followed that with the confusion that always accompanies a transfer. — Looking up officers - packing seabags – saying goodbye, etc. We were on the deck at 1530 ready to go and at 1630 I staggered up the gangway. I mean that literally because I had too heavy seabags and an armful of souvenirs (I am leaving the ship for good)

The Currituck is just like the Pine Island so there is no problem for the location of things . In the evening I went up to the aerological office and got acquainted with Andrews, Hancock and Wilson who went to school with me at Lakehurst. I don't know the other personnel yet.

10 April

(This ship granted liberty at 1300 while the P.I. didn't get it til 1630)
My first complete day aboard the Currituck was one of the utmost ease. I spent it mostly by laying around and getting acquainted with some of the fellows. I also got my first close up of a penguin. We have two of them in a cage on the fantail and although they have a tub of cool running water to bathe in, it's still too hot for them. I understand that we are going to put them in the refrigerator. We had three of them but one male died of a broken heart because the female seemed to prefer the other male. They called for me over the loud speaker about 6:15pm but I was in the balloon shack writing and didn't hear it *(they wanted me for a working party)*.

I went to the movies and hit the sack early because we have to get up early to get underway through the canal. (Coming south to north on the Currituck)

11 April

Stumbled out at 4 o'clock *(woke up 4 or 5 hours later)*. By a little after six we were on our way through the canal. We were supposed to have liberty at 1500 and I was praising the ship as I compared it to the P.I. As the hours rolled around I began to wonder. By the time we got off the base at 1900, I had used a good many bad adjectives referring to the ship. You see we had to be back by 2300 and every minute counted.

I started the evening by almost getting sick on a ham sandwich, a marshmallow sundae, a malted milk, one glass of pineapple juice, and one piece of cherry pie al a mode. I threw that off and we headed into town. We terminated at the Coconut Grove and since it had a continuous floor show we were rather reluctant to leave (*if I didn't think Ma would per chance read this, I might describe the show*). It was pretty high class though.

Took a taxi and was back to the ship 15 minutes early.

12 April

Up at 5 and my peanut brain still can't conceive of any reason for doing it. Hardly had any hangover happily it's because all I had was ice cream.

I don't know how they could do it to me, but they did. I was actually working cleaning the overhead for almost an hour – of course I read the rest of the day.

At 1400 the last liberty before leaving for the states was sounded. I had the duty so you might know that they would give a pretty long liberty.

I sure got a good watch for the $8.50. If I set it every hour I can usually tell within 15 minutes what the time is (*Joe, hand me hammer so I can fix it, but good*).

On the P.I., we usually had the afternoon off on Saturday, however this ship doesn't observe it. It doesn't make any difference to me though, because in aerology we don't work anyway.

13 April

Birthdays today: My cousin Joyce and my Dad.

Well, to celebrate all of the birthdays we started in the last lap of this rat race. Yup, at about 0830 we cast off all lines and headed in a nice northerly direction.

I forgot that this was Sunday so I missed church. I didn't forget that we had holiday routine in the pm, though, so after eating a good chicken dinner I crapped out until supper. (*I forgot to say that we have movies three times on Sunday. Anyway, I went to the one starting at 1 o'clock. I tried to go again at 6 o'clock but the place was too crowded*).

We started our watch schedule which appears to be a good one (*Six sections standing, one four hour watch a day*). I got the 2000 to 2400 with Andrews who went to Lakehurst with me.

14 April

I hate to keep repeating it, but it's true. I didn't do a gosh durn thing today except to stand a two hour watch.

To tell the truth I didn't feel too hot. It was in these waters coming down that I got seasick and I feel a little that way today.

We're bucking a head wind at 25 knots and since the ship is doing 16, that gives an apparent wind of over 40 knots. It's fun walking into it. You can lean over 30 degrees without falling. When you turn your back to it, it sends you slipping and sliding down a spray dampened deck.

We have the pay list up and I noticed that I'm drawing my first clothing allowance. From now on I get 12 bucks extra every three months.

15 April

Ho ho, what's this? Well I'll be gosh durned, they finally put those lazy aerographers to work. Sure enough they had us sweating and puffing as our long unexcersized muscles tried to pass ammunition up four decks. We want to get it handy so it can be taken right off without much fuss in Yorktown.

I'm glad today was payday because I'm almost broke. I drew everything (*$60*) and I hope if I have a leave I'll be able to make it home on the remains of it.

I reduced again by skipping noon chow. (*Of course I had three sundaes and four candy bars to make up for it*).It was probably the last chance to lay in the sun so I took it during noon hour. It was the first time in over a week and a half so most of my tan is gone (*and it used to be so purty*).

16 April

I worked on the working party in the morning, however, I managed to get out of it in the afternoon because I had the watch. LeGrande has been doing alright as far as poker playing since payday is concerned. Yesterday he took in over 400 and tonight his luck failed him when he was only blessed by a couple hundred. That makes almost 2000 he has grossed on the trip. Of course there have been heavier winners but he's doing alright. He's going to buy a car.

It was really hot today and po little me had to stay in the hot office instead of laying in the sun.

I took it easy all night by reading real live, two fisted, rip snorting cowboy stories.

I hear our section has first liberty in Norfolk.

17 April

Had the watch in the am and got on the working party again in the pm. I mailed my seabag home. I had to pull it all apart to be inspected because things have been missing of late.

We made our first step towards hitting port when we got our check-out cards signed. We'll pull in tomorrow.

LeGrande played later last night and won 900 plus at craps. I watched him tonight and he again drew over 550 out of the pot. He really seems to be blessed by good fortune.

I'm afraid I made a pig out of myself by eating 7 ice creams and 4 candy bars. Luckily I'm not sick yet.

It got so cold this morning that I had to use a blanket. I guess we're really getting up north. I see on the map that it's running about freezing at home.

18 April

(one filling fell out)
The first part of the day was like any other with my usual working party. In the afternoon things began to happen. At about 1600 we arrived at pier 4 with cheering crowds around. (*Alright, so there were two women waiting for their husbands*). About 5 o'clock we severed our connections with the Currituck and took a bus to the R/S (reassignment station).

We checked in and had liberty for the night and natch, the ships service was our goal. Believe me, there was a reunion there. It seems that all of the fellows in class 78 that went south had been transferred here. Simpson, Pipenbrink, Andrews, Wilson, Harick, Hancock, Burk, Kyser, Lopp, Scott, Thompson and yours truly. (*A couple others were scattered about*).

After this joyous reunion we saw a new movie with Abbott and Costello (*and the film didn't break*).

Spent the first night ashore in 4 ½ months.

The End

About The Author

Ric* in 2010 (note the hat)

(*When Dick attended Hamilton College, there were several of his dorm mates named Richard, aka Dick. They drew straws for new nicknames, and he's been Ric ever since)

After serving in the US Military, Ric earned his Bachelor's Degree from Hamilton College in Clinton NY. He went on to graduate school, married MaryAnn Scoones and began raising a family. He has four children, Michael, Peter, Paul and Mary Kathryn.

Ric went on to earn a Master's Degree in Math Education from Syracuse University and his Master's Degree in Mathematics from the University of Washington, Seattle.

In 1956 he began teaching at Clarkson College, where he also earned his Ph.D. in Engineering Science. He retired from Clarkson in 1993.

Ric has always been civic minded, giving freely to his community and beyond. He served the West Potsdam fire department for almost 40 years and in 2000, was honored as Fireman of the Year for St. Lawrence County in New York State.

He enjoys reading and learning about the Civil War and has visited Gettysburg and other Civil War sites several times.

An avid reader, Sudoku puzzle solver, coin collector, and other hobbies, Ric entertains his family and friends with stories, facts and information from his varied life experiences.

Known for his ability to recall song lyrics, Ric enjoys listening to music, singing and dancing. For more information about Ric and Operation Highjump, visit:

http://www.ohj.booksforelders.com

The following pages include some of the author's Operation Highjump memorabilia

AGELESS-SAGES.COM PUBLISHING

Tues Dec 3, 1946

Two Local Men on Antarctic Voyage

Two Watertown men are among the 4,000 men who will accompany Rear Admiral Richard E. Byrd on "operation highjump," as it has been called, to explore the Antarctic continent and were aboard ships which sailed Monday on the expedition to explore the earth's last unknown continent around the South Pole.

The men are: Seaman, first class Richard J. Miller, son of Mr. and Mrs. George B. Miller, 419 Broadway avenue west, and Fireman Third Class Robert D. Wells, 17, only son of Mr. and Mrs. Dean J. Wells, 668 Cooper street.

Seaman Miller sailed for the Antarctic on Monday from Norfolk, Va., aboard the U. S. S. Pine Island with Navy task force 68. He recently completed a course in aerography at the Naval Air Station, Lakehurst, N. J.

Before his enlistment in the U. S. Navy last February, Seaman Miller was employed by the Watertown Daily Times in the advertising department.

Fireman Wells is aboard the U. S. S. Yancey, cargo ship, one of the 13 ships which, with the 4,000 men, compose history's greatest Polar expedition. The Yancey left Port Hueneme, Calif., Monday as the peace-time naval task force shoved off for the expedition.

Fireman Wells is a graduate of the North Junior High school and left the Watertown High school to enlist in the U. S. navy last April. After completing preliminary training at Bainbridge, Md., he was assigned to the Yancey. The Yancey, which has been serving in Atlantic waters, left Norfolk, Va., Oct. 23 for the Pacific coast.

Time-Killers on Ship Recounted

Movies Often Interrupted to Push Ice Away from Ships

By FRED SPARKS.

(Special Dispatch to The Watertown Daily Times and The Chicago Daily News.)

Aboard the Icebreaker North Wind, Jan. 14.—Our favorite sport aboard this ship is watching our Helicopter and seaplane return from searches for leads through the Ross sea ice pack.

It's like meeting the once-a-day train at a little rural station. By-standers don't have to ask any questions. They just look at the pilots shaking their heads and know the answer—"the ice ahead is thick, navy bean soup."

Watching penguins is another pleasant time-killer. They line up on an ice floe and dive, chorus style. They make a few circles in the water, then pop back up on the ice like bread out of a toaster.

This is, among other things, the cleanest water in the world. There probably haven't been 50 ships through here since time began. In our own little way we're doing what we can to change that. This troubles 21-year-old Jesus H. Figueroa, of New York.

He watched a load of orange peels, coffee grounds and empty cans being tossed overboard and said: "Soon the seals will think they're swimming at Coney Island."

Sled dogs who live in the fantail of the Mt. Olympus—floating a couple of 100 yards from here—dined deliriously well today on fresh seal meat. Our old friend Jack Perkins, biologist, romped out on the ice and shot one smack in the head.

Seeing a movie aboard the North Wind isn't always very satisfac-tory. The other day, for example, the picture titled, "My Pal Wolf," the story of a brave dog and a lit-tle child, was being shown in the messhall when all hands were called to the deck to help push away ice forming around the mer-rick. The break came just when the villain, a dog catcher, was about to nab the hero, Wolf.

After the ice had been scattered the movie was resumed. But three other times before the finis more ice collected on the other ships and more interruptions resulted. It took almost three and one-half hours to complete the showing of a 70-minute movie. The break always came at the most exciting time, reminding oldsters of the "Perils of Pauline," drama-packed serial of earlier days.

Copyright, 1947, Chicago Daily News, Inc.

Feb 2, 1846

NAVY RECRUITS—Navy recruits who left Wednesday for Albany are shown with Machinist Cyrus H. Osier, recruiter in charge, at the local office in the Federal building, left, and Baker First Class Max E. Ludwick, assistant recruiter, at the right.

Seated are, from left to right: Charles P. Phillipson, 140 North Indiana avenue; Richard J. Miller, 419 Broadway avenue west; Arthur J. Gardner, Natural Bridge; Ellwood D. Demo, Massena.

Standing are: Francis Coughlin, 419 Coffeen street; Benjamin P. Anguliana, 739 West Main street; Cedric M. Forsythe, Natural Bridge; Francis K. Lozo, Natural Bridge, and Edwin J. Barton, Ogdensburg.

—Times Staff Photo

Miller, 3rd from left in front row

126

Cameras Hard To Use at Pole

New York, May 5.—How would you like to operate a camera wearing two pairs of gloves

Or snap a photograph of an iceberg while suspended from a rope over an ice-filled sea that would kill you in five minutes.

Or hike ten miles in a 20-degree-below-zero gale to get a closeup of a seal's head?

Well, those are but a few of the problems that stubborn amateur and professional photographers (including this writer) went through to record pictorially the recent Byrd Antarctic expedition.

The problems of photography in the world of ice and snow called Antartica are without question the most difficult in the world.

Take the average camera, for example. After a few minutes in the sub-zero weather the shutter started to tire as metal contracted and oil froze. Even the navy's cameras, most of which had their oil removed to reduce freezing, slowed from a fox-trot to a waltz. Here's what Lt. Charles Shirley, the energetic photographic officer of the expedition, had to say in his official report:

"It was necessary to advance speed to 1/400ths of a second to obtain a working speed of 1/75ths of a second when the temperature was ten degrees below zero."

Bringing a camera inside your tent was about as simple as bringing a lion up to your hotel room. If you just strolled in the heat from the stove would hit the camera and it would frost over. Then—unless you dashed madly out immediately—the ice, which formed inside the camera as well as outside, would melt and you had the terrific task of taking the entire camera apart to sop up the water.

It was just about impossible to change film wearing the double mittens issued for sub-arctic wear. And if you took your gloves off for even two minutes your hands would become numb. Furthermore you suffered severe metal burns.

U.S. NAVAL ANTARCTIC

TASK GROUP 68.3
CAPTAIN G.J. DUFEK COMMANDING

U.S.S. PINE ISLAND
CAPTAIN H.H. CALDWELL COMMANDING

U.S.S. CANISTEO
CAPTAIN E.K. WALKER COMMANDING

U.S.S. BROWNSON
COMDR. H.M.S. GIMBER COMMANDING

U.S.S. PINE ISLAND (AV-12) FLAGSHIP TG-68.3

U.S.S. BROWNSON (DD-868)

U.S.S. CANISTEO (AO-99)

CAPTAIN G.J. DUFEK & COMDR. H.M.S. GIMBER

COMDR. SCHWARTZ, CAPTAIN DUFEK, CAPTAIN CALDWELL

CONFERENCE AT SEA WITH CAPTAIN WALKER

DEPARTURE DAY - NORFOLK VA.

NEPTUNE'S COURT ABOARD AV-12

JATO TAKE OFF

MIDNIGHT FLIGHT QUARTERS

HOISTING PLANES ABOARD AT NORFOLK

STRAIGHT UP

OPERATION HIGHJUMP

128

City Winter Worse Than at South Pole

Seaman Richard J. Miller Is Back from Trip to Antarctic Regions.

Antarctic winters are not as "tough" as those of the north country, declared Richard John Miller, 19, seaman first class, aerographer's mate in the United States navy, who is back home here after a four-months journey with Admiral Richard E. Byrd's expedition to the South Polar regions.

Seaman Miller, son of Mr. and Mrs. George B. Miller, 419 Broadway avenue west, arrived in Watertown Friday and will remain here on a 20-day leave before returning to navy duty. He served on the aircraft tender, Pine Island, of the eastern group of the Byrd expedition which was mainly utilized in Antarctic coastal exploration work.

The sailor lived for ten weeks aboard the aircraft tender in the Antarctic waters and during the expedition he went for three months without seeing land.

"Although you might not believe it, north country residents had a tougher winter than we did down there," said Seaman Miller. "No below temperatures were encountered on my ship although the temperature on the Antarctic continent did get below zero."

Seaman Miller, formerly employed in the business office of The Watertown Daily Times, enlisted in the navy on March 4, 1946, and studied at Lakehurst, N. J. He volunteered for duty with the Byrd expedition and left on the polar trip last Dec. 2, returning April 18. He remained in the Antarctic operating area from Dec. 23 to March 8.

"My ship didn't see much action inasfar as ice was concerned," said Seaman Miller. "Our mission was to operate outside the ice pack and dispatching of flights whenever weather permitted. However, we did come in contact with ice packs and icebergs, many of which dwarfed the ship. The heaviest ice field was in the Weddell Sea, east of the Palmer peninsula in the Antarctic continent. On the return trip, a propellor of our ship was damaged going through an ice pack."

It was from the aircraft tender, Pine Island, on which the Watertown sailor served, that the plane George 1 took off and later crashed on Cape Dart peninsula. Three men were killed in the crash and eleven others were isolated on an ice shelve for 13 days

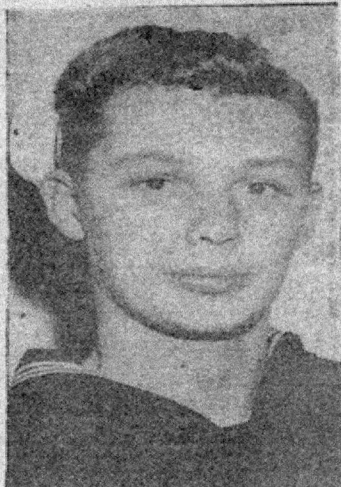
—Times Staff Photo
Seaman R. J. Miller

1946-1947

(?)

U.S.S. PINE ISLAND (AV-12)

FLAGSHIP

Commander Task Group 68.3

SOUTH

U. S. NAVAL ANTARCTIC EXPEDITION

OPERATION HIGHJUMP

TO ALL SAILORS OF THE SEVEN SEAS WHEREVER YE MAY BE:
GREETINGS: *Be it known that*

R. J. MILLER, 239 11 59, S1AERM, U. S. NAVY

while serving aboard the **U.S.S. PINE ISLAND (AV-12)** *on the U. S. Naval Antarctic Expedition 1946-1947*

Transited Panama Canal from Atlantic to Pacific 7 December 1946
Crossed Equator at Longitude 82° 47' West 12 December 1946
Crossed Antarctic Circle at Longitude 99° 44' West 25 December 1946
Southernmost Position Reached at Longitude 69° 55' South 8 February 1947
Rounded Cape Horn from West to East 17 February 1947
Simultaneously crossed Greenwich Meridian and
Antarctic Circle 27 February 1947

H. H. Caldwell

H. H. CALDWELL,
Captain, U.S.N.
Commanding

www.ingramcontent.com/pod-product-compliance
Lightning Source LLC
Chambersburg PA
CBHW030712110426
R18122000003B/R181220PG42736CBX00009B/5